ADVANCE PRAISE FOR

The Courage for Peace

"Excellent. The best book I know on the all-important work that we mediators can—and should—do within ourselves. A first-person account of lessons learned all over the world. It will help you aim high, be open, let go, make room for new understanding, and find an inner peace that will strengthen your ability to build peace with and among others."

> —Roger Fisher, director, Harvard Negotiation Project, coauthor, *Getting to YES*

"This is a rare book distilled from the author's deep and compassionate experience making and building peace at home and abroad. When I read it, I knew I was in the presence of a rare and wise spirit. A must for every peacemaker everywhere."

> —Susan Collin Marks, executive vice president, Search for Common Ground

"We need stories of possibility. We need to understand peace as a personal and collective practice. And we need to place our hands on this book after watching the evening news, and breathe deeply. Louise Diamond helps us remember how to open our minds and hands, so we can reach toward each other in a new way."

> —Dawna Markova, Ph.D., executive thinking partner and author of *The Open Mind, An Unused Intelligence,* and *No Enemies Within*

The Courage for Peace

LOUISE DIAMOND

The Courage for Peace

Creating Harmony in Ourselves and the World

With a New Author's Note

Foreword by Neale Donald Walsch

CONARI PRESS
Berkeley, California

Conari Press books are distributed by Publishers Group West.
Cover photograph by Michael Wilson, courtesy of Swanstock
Cover and book design by Claudia Smelser

LIBRARY OF CONGRESS CATALOGING-IN-PUBLICATION DATA
Diamond, Louise
    The courage for peace : creating harmony in ourselves and the world /
    Louise Diamond : foreword by Neale Donald Walsch.
        p.   cm.
    ISBN: 1-57324-165-2
    1. Peace—religious aspects. I. Title
BL65.P4 D53 2000
291.1'7873—dc21   99–042068

Printed in the United States of America

For my grandchildren, and yours.

THIS BOOK IS DEDICATED TO

My spiritual Teacher, the Venerable Dhyani Ywahoo,

Principal Chief of the Green Mountain Band

Of the Aniyunwiwa (Cherokee) People,

Who is, for me, the Spirit of Peace incarnate.

With boundless compassion and generosity she has passed to me

The precious teachings from her ancient lineage.

They permeate my life and every word in this book.

I am immeasurably grateful.

The Courage for Peace

THREE *Opening the Heart of Peace*

Contents

FOUR *Unleashing the Power of Peace*

FINALE *Finding the Courage for Peace in the
Twenty-First Century*

Call to Action: Peace Resource Guide

Acknowledgments

Author's Note
Making Peace the Way We Live

I WROTE THIS BOOK nearly two years before the world-changing events of September 11, 2001. I believe it is more relevant now than ever.

In these days, when the war on terrorism takes center stage and spreads fear around the globe, humanity is brought quickly to the choice point: How are we to survive—and thrive—as a human family?

How will we find ways to live in harmony and peace despite our differences? How will we care for one another, knowing that the well-being of one depends on the well-being of all? And how will we learn to use and honor our sacred power to create and unite, rather than to dominate and destroy?

I find that people are eager to address these critical questions. We touch on them briefly in our public discourse on politics, the economy, national and world affairs. Yet rarely do we address them head-on, and name them for what they are: the spiritual imperative of our times.

For matters of war and peace are indeed and at core matters of the spirit. When we use violence to harm another, we are destroying part of our own sacred self, for we are one family of life in this universe. Peace is the realization of that oneness; it is a state of union with the divine, made manifest through our relationships with self and others. Our souls hunger for the peace that is our spiritual birthright—a truth that is recognized in virtually all major world religions.

For that reason, I am so pleased to see this One Spirit edition of *The Courage for Peace*. One Spirit readers know that we are cocreating the world we share. They understand that personal responsibility—through clear intention and right action—is the force that shapes our individual and collective lives. They recognize that we are the living seeds of the Spirit of Peace, and that our words and our deeds are expressions of that spirit-in-action.

Because of this, and because of the unique times we face, One Spirit readers are especially attuned to the central message of this book: that **the time has come to make peace the way we live**. We must step away from the story of fear and divisiveness we have allowed our leaders (and a handful of militants) to weave for us, and begin to craft a new story for humanity in which peace—starting with ourselves—is the central organizing principle of our society. This new story is based on hope, not fear; on the best that humanity is capable of, not the worst; on the possibilities that arise when we remember we are all sparks of the one sacred light, that peace is our soul's DNA, and that the potential to actualize that peace resides within each and every one of us.

The Courage for Peace is a road map for this journey. It tells the stories of individuals around the world who have found concrete and practical ways to awaken and embody the Spirit of Peace in themselves and others. It also lays out the basic spiritual principles that guide this journey. Most importantly, the book is a reaffirmation that each and every one of us CAN make a positive difference in a post-9/11 world.

I strongly believe the times compel us to remember our spiritual duty. We are here to make "Peace on Earth" a dream come true. Now, more than ever we need to engage our body, mind and spirit toward that goal. I pray that *The Courage for Peace* may serve as an invitation and an inspiration for you, dear reader, to walk the peace path—for the benefit of all our relations and all our tomorrows.

Louise Diamond
Lincoln, Vermont
September 2004

Foreword

by Neale Donald Walsch

A FEW YEARS AGO I wrote a trilogy of books under the title *Conversations with God* that caught the attention of a significant audience, numbering in the millions worldwide, and that has prompted a question I am asked over and over again, wherever I go.

"We are so inspired by what was contained in those books," this question usually begins, then continues, "but how can we apply these spiritual principles to our daily lives? For that matter, is this even possible? Are they even practical?"

I've always thought they were, of course, although many of the concepts contained in *Conversations with God* certainly seem impractical to a great many people when challenged to apply them. "There's no such thing as Right and Wrong," "There are no victims and there are no villains," "No one does anything inappropriate, given their model of the world," and other pronouncements may appear to be good ideas between the covers of a book, but in actual human relationships—not to mention relations between nations—they can be a bit tricky.

And as for the central, overarching message of the entire trilogy—"We are all One"—that can be the trickiest of all to fit into our day-to-day scheme of things.

Yet, says *Conversations with God,* until we find a way to apply this wisdom, and make it work, ours will remain an essentially primitive society. And finding that way may not be easy, given the cultural myths we have allowed to inform our decisions on this planet. Chief among these is the "every man for himself/survival of the fittest" myth that has us honoring rugged individualism to the near-total exclusion of any kind of unification philosophy that would allow us to join together in certain causes for the common good, and the reductionist myth that has us continuing to solve the mysteries of life by reducing every system we see to its smallest parts in order to understand its mechanics, to the near-complete exclusion of any approach that would allow us to see that none of the mechanics work unless all of the smallest parts fit together.

It is going to take determined and widespread leadership for the human race to overcome these myths—a new kind of army, in fact. An army for peace.

Because peace is what we are talking about here. Everything that robs us of our peace springs from one of these two myths: the idea that we are separate from each other, and the idea that everything in life is best understood by reducing it to its smallest parts and analyzing how they work. This Separatist/Reductionist philosophy is what is killing us—and I've used that term advisedly. It is, quite literally, killing us. From Kosovo to our own schoolyards, we are killing each other out of our thought that we are disconnected from each other in our Being and in our Doing—when, in fact, we are not. We are One Being operating in a Whole System, but we seem unable or unwilling to see that, much less to respond to its most obvious implications: that what we do to each other we are doing to ourselves, and what we fail to do for each other we fail to do for ourselves.

What will it take for us to turn things around, before we "reduce" ourselves to nothing, and "separate" ourselves from Life itself? *Conversations with God* makes it very clear. "It will take courage." It is never popular to act out of accordance with the prevailing cultural myth. Yet act out of accordance we must, if we are to survive our own greatest misunderstandings.

Fortunately, there appears to be a growing will to do so. The human race is losing patience with itself—and that is a very good sign. We are, most of us, beginning to see that the way we've been going about things has not been working. We may still not be clear about which way *will* work, but we are becoming very clear about which way will not. More and more of us are shaking our heads, agreeing, "There must be a better way." In our personal lives, in our corporate affairs, in our political machinations, in our international interactions, there must be a better way, a more peaceful way, to create and experience our lives.

Foreword

There is. And now Louise Diamond, in *The Courage for Peace,* has given us a path that we might follow, a way that we might arrive at the place where we all say that we want to be. This is wonderful news; this is wonderful reading. Here are practical examples, real-life stories of how real-life people have lived the real truth of how Life really is— that we *are* all One, that this *is* a Whole System, and that there *is* a way to live together in harmony, and in peace.

Thank you, Louise Diamond, for this clarion call. Thank you for showing us that there is a way that we can take the highest spiritual principles understood by human beings and apply them to everyday life. Thank you for letting us see that all it takes is *the courage for peace.*

Releasing the Spirit of Peace

AN ANGRY SOLDIER was waving an automatic weapon in my face, but I was too indignant to be afraid. I had been in a small shop near the main marketplace of a city long embittered by ethnic conflict. Suddenly I heard the unmistakable and all too familiar sounds of a violent demonstration outside. The streets were filled with shouts and popping sounds, and with people running for safety, pursued by irate soldiers. Whiffs of tear gas drifted in from the central square. Everyone in the shop ran to the door to see what was happening.

Abruptly, a group of soldiers appeared at the doorstep. In the whirl of confusion that followed, a young man who had been in the shop with me was grabbed by the soldiers and whisked off to detention. We shouted after them, "Why are you taking him?" "He threw rocks at us," the soldiers replied, "and participated in the demonstration just now. He must be jailed, to teach them all a lesson."

Since all of us in the shop were witness to the young man's presence with us during the events in the street, we knew he could not possibly be guilty of what the soldiers were accusing him. We also knew, the locals more immediately than I, that this information would mean nothing to the authorities. Having grabbed a "troublemaker," they could keep him imprisoned for months or even years, without formal charges or court proceedings.

The people around me became more and more agitated, and began chasing the soldiers, demanding the release of their compatriot. As an outsider, I saw I might have a special opportunity to defuse the tension and encourage a nonviolent response. I went with the group through the narrow, crowded streets to the detention area in which they were holding the dozens of "troublemakers" rounded up on this occasion. Stepping in front of the restless crowd, I addressed the soldiers guarding the gate and politely asked for the release of this particular young man, giving my evidence of his innocence.

"Go away," shouted the soldier who seemed to be in charge, pointing his AK47 at me. "You don't belong here." I continued my plea, committed to a peaceful and fair outcome in this extremely volatile and dangerous situation. The soldier replied even more vehemently, "Go away! What happened here today doesn't concern you. You are a foreigner; what business is it of yours?" "I am a human being," I answered, with as much dignity and authority as I could muster, "and this is human business." Within the hour, the young man was released.

How did I, an ordinary American woman, come to find myself in such a situation? Where in my life's journey did I learn that peace is not just human business, but specifically my business, my calling? My career development began naturally enough. A master's degree in English led to teaching at a small-town high school in northern Vermont. The Vermont Department of Education was looking for people to work with its drug education program in 1970, and I was hired. That work took me into the area of human behavior, and soon I was offering training, running groups, and working with private clients as a psychotherapist and an organizational consultant.

In the ensuing years, I found that whether I was working with individuals, couples, families, or organizations, the work was inevitably about issues of power and healing. In short, people were struggling to find peace and balance within themselves, and to live and work harmoniously with each other. Many of the people I came in contact with had been deeply wounded or traumatized, emotionally and sometimes physically. Some were suicidal, and at least one potentially homicidal.

Problems I encountered within families ranged from mild distress to extreme expressions of rage and anguish. Some of the organizations I consulted with were bogged down in the worst kind of power struggles and divisiveness. All those years, unbeknownst to myself, I was preparing to meet the larger world of international ethnic conflict through exposure to a whole range of human experience and behavior rooted in distrust, pain, and fear.

Two episodes of cancer and one motorcycle crash brought me face to face with my own healing journey, which also expanded my work in the world. Soon I was also acting as a spiritual and healing guide with people who had severe and often terminal illnesses or major mental disturbances. Then, more than a decade ago, my spiritual evolution brought me to peace work at a higher level, and I began to act as a third-party peacebuilder in places of ethnic and communal violence around the world.

I began traveling to the Middle East, and made a film about the Israeli-Palestinian conflict. Soon I was involved also with conflicts in Cyprus, Bosnia, Liberia, the Horn of Africa, India-Pakistan, and elsewhere—places where colonialism, ethnic divisions, war, and atrocities had left deep scars and fears for the future. In bringing people from all walks of life together across "enemy" lines for dialogue, problem solving, and reconciliation in these settings, I have been privileged to encounter some truly remarkable human beings grappling—with varying degrees of success—with truly difficult and often dangerous situations. It is through this spectrum of my own work and life experience that I came to know that peace is, indeed, the business of all human beings.

Peace everywhere, at home and abroad, is our common human concern. Making peace or finding peace or building peace are activities we each need to do every single day of our ordinary lives. In our daily lives with children and parents, partners and friends, colleagues and neighbors, we are engaged in the human business of peace. If we want inner serenity, if we want happy and healthy relationships with those we love, we are concerned with peace. If the quality of life in our workplace and community is important to us, we are concerned with peace. If we care about the well-being of our natural environment, of our economic and political climate, or of the nations of the world, we are necessarily concerned with peace.

Peace, then, is the everyday practical matter of how we can live together harmoniously, dealing creatively and effectively with the inevitable differences, hurts, and fears that arise in human relationships. It is also a spiritual ideal that has inspired human beings throughout time and across cultures. On a larger scale, peace is a political goal of nations and peoples; on a smaller scale, inner peace is a personal goal for those of us who are trying to live more consciously within this frenzied world. Spiritual, political, practical, and personal—peace is important in all these dimensions, and affects us all.

One situation in particular, many years ago, convinced me of this universal nature of peace, and opened the door through which the seed of this book blew into my soul. I was facilitating a dialogue between Israelis and Palestinians near Jerusalem.

"Why are you here?" I queried, curious to know what motivated people to take the personal and political risks of meeting one another across "enemy" lines.

"Because I know there has to be a better way," answered one of the participants, a woman whose life had been defined in many ways by the ongoing violence in the region.

"How do you know, how can you know about this better way, when you and your family have lived only in conflict for so many years, decades, even generations?" I responded.

Putting her hand to her heart and tapping gently, she replied with firm assurance, "I know; I just know."

I have seen countless variations of this scenario over the years. People affected by some of our world's most bitter conflicts have come together with their so-called enemies to begin the long, slow process of reconciliation, often putting themselves in great danger by doing so.

Releasing the Spirit of Peace

When asked what moves them to take this courageous step, they invariably touch their hearts and affirm a "knowing" deep inside that there is a better way, that peace is possible.

Where does that "knowing" come from? I believe it is encoded within us, embedded in the spiritual template of our souls. We are wired for Peace with a capital P, much like we are wired for certain physical traits through our DNA structure. In the same way, we are preset for other ideals as well, such as Love, Justice, Mercy, Truth, Freedom, and Beauty.

Throughout history, humanity has unwaveringly pursued these values. While the particular manifestation of each ideal may change with culture or time, the yearning for them seems to be an innate part of the human experience.

I believe we are born with this inner potential for peace; it lies within our very nature, waiting to be awakened and enlivened by our will. We can choose to free it as a living force that brings joy and harmony to our families, our communities, our nation, and our planet. Or we can choose to ignore it, leaving it as buried treasure, to be uncovered some later day.

Over the years, I have come to have great respect for this living force, and have found it to have both a name and a power that can change the world. I call it the Spirit of Peace.

The Spirit of Peace is familiar to us through the actions of many inspirational figures throughout history. When we acknowledge Christ as the Prince of Peace; when we honor the nonviolent approaches of Mahatma Gandhi, Martin Luther King, Jr., or His Holiness the Dalai Lama; when we are touched by the deep compassion of Mother Theresa for the poor of India; when we marvel at the courage of

Anwar Sadat on his groundbreaking trip to Jerusalem—we are witnessing the Spirit of Peace in human form. The wonderful news is that we don't have to be a "saint" to embody it—each of us has complete access to that same power in our daily lives.

I've found that the Spirit of Peace is not some divine presence that will descend from the heavens to make everything miraculously right, but rather is an innate potential within our human experience, which can be awakened and engaged in the messy process of righting our broken relationships. It is the life force within that template, the living power of Peace that resides in every human heart, as available as the breath, as constant as the pulsing heartbeat.

I don't remember an exact moment when I discovered the Spirit of Peace inside my own heart. Like a photograph being developed, it came gradually into focus, a presence in my life, until it seemed there was never a time when it wasn't there.

Sometimes I experience the Spirit of Peace as a protective friend, like a guardian angel; sometimes as a teacher, guiding my words and action. It may feel at times like a "she"; at other times like a "he"; and sometimes like a neutral but potent force or energy.

Often I experience the Spirit of Peace as the Divine Mystery, manifest in one of its several robes. It is the realization of the promise, held by many of the world's major religions, that we are made in the image of God. It is an expression of our own divine nature, our inherent wholeness.

I have developed an intimate relationship with this sacred friend. I tell him how my work is going, ask her for guidance, put the hard cases into his capable hands, cry to her for help, invite him to speak and act through me.

Recently I've begun to notice how the Spirit of Peace walks and talks in the world around me, especially in situations of deprivation, fear, conflict, and woundedness; how it shows itself in the minds and actions of others. I've started to pay attention to where and how this energy can be consciously evoked, intentionally called forth.

By tapping her heart and affirming her knowledge of "a better way," the woman in that Israeli-Palestinian dialogue made a connection with this natural source of power, and began the journey to release that Spirit of Peace into everyday reality.

This book is about that journey. We do not have to live in Kosovo or Rwanda to seek the Spirit of Peace. Right here in the United States we need its help. In our personal lives, in our communities, in our places of work and play and worship, in our public and political lives and in our institutions, we are in desperate need of finding a better way to relate to one another. We all need to recognize ourselves as peacebuilders, for the brokenness of the world appears not only in war zones but in our own back yards.

We have become a violent society. We glorify violence in our media, programming our children and our citizenry through daily exposure to television shows, movies, computer games, books, newscasts, and toys that display violence as a suitable or even "cool" way of solving our problems. We have the most highly armed citizenry, the greatest per capita numbers of prison inmates (with a shocking growth in the numbers of young children convicted of violent crimes), and the highest incidence of capital punishment in the industrial world, and we are proud of these "accomplishments."

We have become an adversarial society. We take a strong stance of "us" against "them" in our social and political institutions, polarizing ourselves into factions that seek to figuratively (and sometimes literally) dominate or destroy each other. Whether the "they" are immigrants, those who disagree with our views on abortion or environmental matters, members of another political party, or people who are different from us in any number of ways, a combative stance has become our social norm. This stance shows up in our civil discourse, which has become decidedly uncivil—full of rudeness, name calling, and disrespect in our families, schools, and streets, and even in our loftiest political institutions.

Our adversarial mindset leads us to argument as a way of life. We revere debate as a form of both communication and entertainment. We pride ourselves on our ability to argue endlessly, institutionalizing and legitimating this process through our over-reliance on the confrontational and litigious system of the courts. We even argue with ourselves, doing battle with our own nature as we agonize over our self-worth, our lovableness, or our body image.

We have become a divided society, with historical rifts between various racial and ethnic groups that have never healed, and increasing economic divisions between the "haves" and the "have nots." Underlying those rifts are belief systems that, positing the superiority of one group over another, tear at the fabric of our society. Embedded in so many of our institutions, they feed a structural violence that undermines our moral integrity as a nation, and diminishes our human resource capacity.

Finally, we have become a greedy society. Shopping, the accumulation of materials goods, and investing, the accumulation of financial gain, have become our national pastimes. In our rush to satisfy our material cravings, we have forgotten that life has a higher meaning. We ignore the relationship between our having a life of ease and comfort, and the living and working conditions of the people who make the goods we so covet, who live in less affluent parts of the world. In our rush for buying and owning, we conveniently overlook the drain our "having" puts on the Earth's limited and decreasing supply of natural resources, which, in our arrogance, we assume exist primarily for our enrichment and pleasure. This same attitude allows us to step over the pain of our most vulnerable members—our poor, our elderly, our immigrants, our homeless, our disabled, our ill—and do little to help them, thinking, I suppose, some version of, "I've got mine; they'll have to get theirs however they can."

These conditions are not benign. Taken together, they are shockingly similar to some of the patterns we see in places of violent conflict around the world. I'm not suggesting the United States will necessarily dissolve into chaos and warfare. Nonetheless, by allowing these conditions to flourish, we are making ourselves vulnerable to the kinds of destructive forces that have ravaged places like Bosnia, Somalia, and Rwanda.

Life in our society has become like a battlefield, and in that battle we have forgotten what we have always known instinctively—that there is, truly, a better way; a better way to live together, a better way to cherish one another, a better way to honor our sacred potential, a better way to serve the life force, a better way to build peace into the fabric of our lives.

This book is an attempt to reflect on that better way. It is a journey of our collective heart and soul, seeking to discover the Spirit of Peace in action. For some, this may seem like a huge and hopeless task. The forces at play appear too big; we as individuals feel too small. What can one person do against these deeply embedded societal patterns?

I am familiar with this sense of helplessness. I am also aware that it feeds the status quo. No one of us needs to carry the burden of social transformation alone. Each one of us can find the Spirit of Peace in our own lives, and invite it to blossom in our own unique circumstances, touching our family, friends, coworkers, and neighbors like the ripples from a pebble tossed into the water. Each one of us can find that better way for ourselves, and in doing so, participate in the healing of our broken world.

I believe our planet is facing a major crossroad, a critical choice point in human history, where the choices we make now will determine the very survival of our species. These choices have to do with how we manage the seeming paradox that we are a single family of life on this planet, yet with a multiplicity of differences.

Somehow, we must find a way to honor both that unity and that diversity within the precious, fragile web of Earth's interdependence. This will require great courage, for it means a thorough reexamination of our motivations, our behaviors, and our institutions. I trust, I know, that the Spirit of Peace can help us make these choices, so that we can find a better way to treat one another and to structure our relationships at the personal, group, and global levels.

My spiritual teacher of more than twenty years, the Venerable Dhyani Ywahoo, says that there are many great beings in other dimensions just waiting for a catalytic number of people to be awakened to their potential as co-creative beings, waiting for the invitation to be of great service to humanity in these times. I believe that the Spirit of Peace is one of these beings, who already dwells within our highest selves and can be called to fuller presence by our collective yearning. I offer this book as part of that invitation.

Releasing the Spirit of Peace

If we can invoke and evoke this Spirit of Peace in our lives, then the true miracle of peace can cut through the seemingly impossible knots that bind human relationships into the twisted and sorry shapes we see on television every night. If we call her, she will come—arising from our hearts and moving through our lives as an outpouring of harmony, reconciliation, and healing.

To call forth the Spirit of Peace, we must ask the same questions of ourselves that those Israeli and Palestinian peacebuilders faced that day in dialogue: "If there is a 'better way' to manage our relationships, what is it? How do we 'know' it and find it in our hearts, and make it real in our lives—personally, politically, practically, and spiritually?"

The road map I have found to that "better way" lies in four simple spiritual lessons, four principles that, through both faith and common sense, show us a clear path to peace. These lessons have to do with our basic unity and wholeness; our interdependence; the power of love for reconciliation; and our ability, through conscious thought and action, to shape the world we live in.

I've chosen to write this book as an inquiry into the practical implications of these spiritual lessons. There is much we do not yet know about the Spirit of Peace. If we knew how to heal ancient wounds and restore justice, if we knew how to ensure happy families and healthy communities, we would have done so. What is Peace? What is Right Relationship? What is Reconciliation? What is Peacebuilding? These questions are on the growing edge of our human understanding; they pose our evolutionary challenge.

In this book we will explore these questions through the experiences of many who have known the Spirit of Peace. Their stories, their tales, speak through voices woven together like the instruments of a symphony orchestra. The first of these voices is that of the Spirit of Peace, acting as the underlying drumbeat, providing us with a rhythm and pulse to our inquiry. This presence speaks through a short poem at the beginning of each chapter, and through the explanation of each of the four spiritual lessons.

The second voice is that of everyday peacebuilders, adding their song over the basic rhythm. People from all walks of life who have felt the Spirit of Peace move in their lives—in our schools and neighborhoods, our workplaces and our streets, or in places of deep-rooted violence around the world—share their stories. These stories speak boldly about the capacity of the human spirit in times of adversity, and give concrete examples of what is possible.

The continuing story line of my own journey as a peacemaker is a third voice, deepening the inquiry through an exploration of my particular understanding, gained through direct experience. Finally, there is the voice of reflection, in simple essay form, providing a melody of commentary to explore further the ideas raised by the stories.

In a symphony, each movement ends with a recapitulation of the theme. At the end of each chapter, then, I reexamine the essential wisdom explored in the chapter, and offer two simple exercises to apply that wisdom to our everyday lives—one inner or meditative practice, and one action-oriented practice. For the Spirit of Peace is about action; it is about concretely manifesting in our lives and in our world that "better way" of being together.

By using this format, I am making two assumptions. One is that the work of peacebuilding is the same work, dealing with essentially the same dynamics and processes, whether it is occurring at the individual, interpersonal, group, intergroup, or international level. Thus, when we read a story from any one of those categories, we can understand it as a metaphor for all the others, and make the translation in our own minds. A story about civil strife in Bosnia, for instance, might open our eyes to what's happening in our neighborhoods, or an incident between mother and daughter can teach us much about the nature of the relationship between our political parties.

The second assumption I make is that certain basic truths inform (literally, give form to) our lives and choices. I think of this as an "if. . . , then. . ." rather than a "how to" book. If each spiritual lesson is true, then certain other ideas and actions naturally follow. Our beliefs imply particular behaviors, and have natural and logical consequences.

To walk this path, with the Spirit of Peace, is not an easy way, for it commits us to daily acts of difficult choice. Applying the lessons in our lives means examining our motivations, feelings, and behaviors. It means questioning our leaders, our institutions, and our assumptions about how we live together in our communities and in our world. To walk this path is to face societal pressures that would maintain a status quo grounded in competition, aggression, and adversarial thinking, and still do things differently. To walk this path is to display the courage for peace.

To ensure the safety of some of the brave peacebuilders whose stories told here exemplify this courage, I have at times changed or omitted identifying data or crafted a composite of various incidents. Yet all the stories tell the essential truth of their experience. Through these tales and musings, I hope to pose the provocative questions, and tap the elemental principles that will reveal more fully the living presence of Peace.

Writing this book has been a joy for me. I have particularly delighted in imagining my partners in this inquiry, you who are reading these words, whoever you are, in all your divine beauty. I hope that this experience will be fruitful for you, and that you find at least one small gem that will enrich your life and the lives of those you touch.

I hope that this book can help you find your own direct access to the Spirit of Peace, that template in the heart of universal knowing, for once you know the way home, you can go there whenever you want. Perhaps we can meet there, discovering together the treasure of peace in our lives this very moment, and creating a world beyond violence, where our children and grandchildren can live peace-fully in spirit and action. That is my prayer and my offering.

ONE

Come, let us go home
Where one peace warms us all
at the same fire.

Tapping the Source of Peace

It's in the Blood

SOME OF US need a strong wake-up call before we can give our attention to the Spirit of Peace. I am one of those sluggards. I needed to be vigorously shaken out of my complacency not once, but twice, with a direct confrontation with death, before I recognized the call.

My journey as a peacebuilder began with the flowing of my own blood. In 1973, at age twenty-eight, I had my first mastectomy for breast cancer. Newly divorced, a single mother with an energetic toddler,

I faced my mortality for the first time. Nine months later, a tumor in the other breast led to a near-death experience during my second mastectomy operation. My medical chances of surviving these two rounds of cancer were, I discovered later, in the 0 percent range.

I remember when the hysteria set in. Shortly after I returned from the hospital after the second operation, I received a birth announcement in the mail. My instinctive reaction was, "It's not fair! How can my friends be celebrating new life when I'm preparing for death?"

Then the memories started, and the weeping. I began to relive my near-death experience of the week before, when I had bled to the very point of death on the operating table. Though I had been anesthetized for the operation, my cellular memory was keen.

I thought I was going crazy, as the hours passed and I remained hysterical. I now know the meaning of the expression, "bouncing off the walls." I literally threw myself from one corner to the next, wailing and screaming. I was not dealing with conscious thoughts; I was not crying "about" anything. I was re-experiencing the bloody passing of my life force as I howled, over and over again, "The blood! The blood!"

After two days of this, with little food or rest, I finally exhausted myself. My friends, frightened that I was in fact losing my mind, loaded my limp body into a car and drove me to a therapist. Their timing couldn't have been better. I was drained, I was empty; I was ready to fill again.

In a later interview, the therapist acknowledged to me his profound fear in that moment. He, like everyone else around me, assumed I was dying. He had no idea what to say to me; in fact, he was concerned that whatever he said could make things worse. He abandoned, therefore, his need to "do the right thing" and simply spoke the words that came through. He said later that the words surprised him as much as they did me.

His unexpected words provided a pivot in my life, and opened the door to the Spirit of Peace. He said, "So you're going to die. So what? Everyone is going to die. Maybe you have a better idea of how and when than most of us. Maybe not. You could outlive us all. Or you could leave this office and be hit by a car.

"If you want to feel sorry for yourself, I'm sure you have many friends who will join you with their pity. But there is another way to think about this. Imagine that Death, which is present for all of us, is just over your shoulder. Don't ask if you're going to die, or when; ask yourself how you want to be when Death comes for you. That's all. Now get out of here."

In that moment, the shape of my entire world shifted. I realized, "How I want to be when Death comes for me is full of joy, full of love, full of peace, full of life. Since I don't know the moment that Death will come, I will have to live this way in every moment, no matter how many moments I have in this life. I choose to do this." It was that simple and that revolutionary. I left the office physically and emotionally numb, but spiritually humming.

As that seed germinated during the next days and months, I realized that, having set the intention for living fully in each moment, I had neither the experience to do so, nor any role models to follow. Finding no human teachers who, in my view, had mastered the art of living this passionately, I turned to the natural world for lessons about the nature and mysteries of life.

During the next four years, I spent as much time as possible in nature. In the forests, fields, and mountains of Vermont, I rediscovered the original miracle of life. By the rivers, ponds, and beaches of New England, I was reborn and baptized into true joy. In the canyons, deserts, and mesas of the southwest, I found stillness and deep inner peace. My elemental soul was revealed to me by the sun and the rocks, through cloud and wind, in the soil and mud of the Earth herself. I found love among the bees and hummingbirds of the orchards, the frogs and the skimmers of the marsh, the deer and the snakes of the woodlands.

During this outer discovery, I was also looking deep within. All the patterns in my life not aligned with my new intention came to the surface to be transformed. Thus I had the opportunity to reexamine all my relationships, starting with my relationship with myself. How I felt about my body, my sexuality, my sense of worth and lovableness; beliefs about my competence; questions about the purpose of my life; how I dealt with my emotions—these were the threads of the old tapestry I was beginning to unravel.

My relationships with others—with parents, family, lovers, friends—also came up for scrutiny. Relationships to work, to action, to community life went under the microscope. Ultimately, the critical issue was about my relationship to God, to Spirit, to my own divine and sacred Self.

While these questions exist along the entirety of my life path, they were particularly intense for me during that period. I experienced this time as a spiritual Roto-Rooter, in which all the gunk built up in my heart flow and mind stream over the years was scoured out by the driving commitment I had made, and needed to reaffirm daily, to live a better way.

Through this unfolding, I realized that I am indeed one with all that is; that every aspect of creation is my relative, and that my thoughts, feelings, and actions affect the entire web of life. In other words, I grew up, and took responsibility for what and how I am creating with every breath. The implications of these lessons led inexorably to one conclusion: I live in service to the whole.

That vow began my peace ministry, and answered the question of why, at the point of death, I was sent back from the Light by a voice that said, "It's not time yet; you have much to do."

My own case was extreme. I had to face death, and my fear of it, before I could claim life fearlessly. Now, in retrospect, I can see that what I am calling the Spirit of Peace was there in the blood all the time, waiting to be liberated. For me, that meant a literal flowing and cleansing of the life force, so that a more vital stream could course through me.

Not everyone has such a dramatic turning point. But everyone does have moments in their lives when conditions are ripe for choosing to do things differently. In those moments, the door is open to tap into the Source of our inner wisdom and to find a new level of inner peace, a new availability to love and joy. Perhaps the secret of peace is to be able to recognize, and take advantage of, those precious moments.

Spiritual Lesson 1:
The One That We Are Is Simply Divine!

Western culture teaches us that we are separate from the rest of creation, that we stand alone in a mostly hostile, occasionally friendly world. In the United States, some of our strongest national myths are expressions of this belief: we honor the rugged individual, the lonesome cowboy, the Lone Ranger. We speak of the struggle of man against nature. We celebrate our conquest of space and of the Wild West.

Conflict simply heightens this view. When we are in a dispute with someone, we see that person as "other" than us. We notice and experience the differences, and polarize these as "right" and "wrong," or "better" and "worse." (We, of course are right and better; the "other" is wrong and worse.) The last thing we want, in the middle of a "good" fight, is to think about our shared essence. Yet that shared essence, our oneness, is the unremembered truth of our being.

Our natural and physical sciences, major faith traditions, and renowned philosophers, poets, and shamans have described this phenomenon of oneness in various ways. We might understand that we are all part of the same Creation. We might believe in one God, one Source, a single spiritual force or power that goes by many names. Or we might describe our unity as the interdependence of all life on this planet, or in the universe.

Some have experienced the oneness as a mystical union with the divine, as a sexual union with our beloved, as a financial union of the global marketplace, or as a communications union in cyberspace. Certainly the now-famous photograph of the Earth from space is a bright reminder that our political and religious differences are arbitrary and unnecessary divisions on this single lovely planet that we all inhabit together.

We experience oneness when we realize that all human beings have the same emotions and aspirations; that no one wants to suffer; that all want to live happily, in peace and freedom. Or we can experience that oneness when we look at one another and see a brother or sister in the single family of life, regardless of nationality, race, lifestyle, or creed.

However we come to it, the basic spiritual truth of our existence is that we are one. There are, it seems to me, several aspects of this oneness that are important: We share the same essence; that essence is divine; we are part of the larger whole of creation, naturally connected to all the other parts; and we carry the seed or potential of that whole within us, like an acorn carries the potential of the oak.

The Judeo-Christian heritage says that we are created in the image of God. Buddhism says all beings are inherently endowed with basic Buddha nature. Native American spirituality posits the sacredness and interconnectedness of all life. Many spiritual paths speak of the one Light, understanding light as the basic medium of our divine nature.

From whatever tradition we choose, the message is the same: Though our outward appearances are vastly different, we are each, at our core, a manifestation of the same sacred spark of life. We are unique, but our being transcends our uniqueness. We are each an integral and necessary part of something larger, higher, than our individual selves.

Modern science teaches us that the part contains the whole. Our universe is a holographic set of nested systems. That is, whether we focus on a single cell, a social group, or a star system, we are really looking at the whole of creation. The microcosm and macrocosm are one. From subatomic particle to huge families of whirling galaxies, we are dealing with the same patterns and principles of energy in motion, the same inherent mystery, the same holy essence.

In alchemical terms, this truth is expressed in the phrase, "As above, so below." If we each contain the whole of creation, then we contain all the inherent potential of its sacred completeness. All the qualities that we ascribe to the Godhead, however we understand that, are also in us. Our true nature and the true nature of the cosmos are the same.

Just because we may not be aware, through our limited senses of perception, of the more subtle and invisible elements of this wholeness, does not mean they do not exist, or are not available to us through other doorways, like prayer and meditation.

New physics teaches us that all phenomena are both a particle and a wave simultaneously; that is, we are both individual and part of a larger flow, like being a single drop of water and at the same time an indistinguishable part of the vast and endless ocean. The problem arises when we think of ourselves only as one or the other.

If we look to ourselves as particles, or individuals, we fail to see our unity with the whole, and we fall prey to all the ills of separation—loneliness, grasping, aggressiveness, pride. If we look to ourselves as only the wave, or group, we fail to notice the uniqueness of our differences, and the special gifts that each one brings to the whole. In this case, we fall prey to all the ills of overgeneralization—arrogance, totalitarianism, extremism, intolerance. We are called to honor our individuality and diversity within the context of the Oneness.

This unity runs like an underground stream beneath our feet. We may not always be aware of it, but when we are thirsty and find a fresh spring bubbling up from the Earth, we are grateful to drink. Just as we thirst for water, so our souls thirst to remember the bottomless pool of our true and holy nature, the infinite ocean of our inherent wisdom.

There are countless ways to recall this connection. Music, poetry, dance, drumming, communing with nature, making love, deep relaxation, finding the "zone" in sports, prayer, and meditation are common avenues. Some of us have learned to invoke our higher power, to call forth our inner wisdom, to listen to the "still small voice within."

The methods are varied; the result is the same. When we connect to this place—whether we call it God, Allah, the Life Force, Light, Great Spirit, Great Mother, Divine Mystery, Yah, Pure Energy, Holy Spirit, or whatever—we feel empowered, safe, vital, loved, and loving. When we tap into that energy, we have access to vision, intuition, creativity, synergy, and the power of miracles—resources of mind, body, and spirit far beyond our day-to-day awareness. When we rest there, we are at home; we have found inner peace.

The Spirit of Peace arises from this place. Our work, when confronted with our small-minded sense of separation, our lack of harmony, our experience of conflict, is to center home, to return to this place of peace and power, and to let that remembrance awaken what we need to carry us to a new level of thought and action.

What Is Peace?

Peace is like a river, running silent and deep, or like the moon's reflection on the water in a sparkling path of light. For some, peace is a sense that all's well with the world. For others, it is the image of a circle of joined hands, people of all colors standing together for love and justice.

In the field of Peace Studies, the conventional wisdom is that we must distinguish between negative peace and positive peace. Negative peace is the absence of war, the cessation of violent hostilities. This is not negative in the sense of "bad," but rather as a photographic negative—the necessary first step to the production of the final image. Positive peace presupposes this cease-fire status, and implies a more active pursuit of a dynamic state of social and economic justice, environmental integrity, human rights, and empowered processes of governance and development for the benefit of all, not merely a privileged few.

Many people associate the word *peace* with weakness. Peace means surrender or being a wimp, a collapse into some amorphous "feel good" place. Others allow historical and political connotations to cloud their associations with peace. Someone once told me that *peace* was a dirty word for him, because, while he and his generation had fought honorably and courageously against tyranny in World War II, his sons and others in the next generation, by opposing the Vietnam War, had defiled the concept of the noble soldier who serves the cause of peace.

Everyone naturally brings their own experiences to their understanding of peace. For me, peace is literally a powerhouse of strength. I experience peace as a specific vibration or dynamic state of being, which, like a song, radiates from my heart and soul.

Synonyms of the word *peace* in my thesaurus point in three directions: one having to do with order, harmony, and unity; one having to do with calm, tranquility, and equanimity; and one having to do with agreement, accord, and rapport. We might call these the "metaphysical" stream, the "serenity" stream, and the "relationship" stream of peace.

I make sense of these three streams by thinking of the metaphysical element as the ground from which the other two arise. That is, the order, harmony, and unity of all creation is the basis for the highest order of peace, the wellspring or Source from which we can draw to know true peace. From that place arises the opportunity for both inner and outer peace, that is, serenity within ourselves and the ability to be in right relationship with others.

The Spirit of Peace reminds us that the three work together. One without the others is incomplete. Inner peace is based on awareness of that essential, universal wholeness. Peace in our relationships is sustained by our ability to tap into, and move from, that place of inner peace. Our spiritual progress as human beings, individually and collectively, is to bring that natural order into concrete form and action in our lives, "on earth as it is in heaven."

Motivation Matters

When people come to me to talk about creating peace in their lives, they want to change. But change is not always easy. We human beings are creatures of habit. We generate patterns of thought and action, and then we reproduce those patterns until, like a river moving in a streambed through rock, we feel trapped in a narrow valley, rushing heedlessly along a course that seems both inevitable and unstoppable.

Even when our path carries us in a direction that is hurtful, even when it takes us away from the light and further into the shadows of our pain, we stay with what we know. In fact, we often take ourselves to the depths of our suffering before we are ready to reach out for change. We tend to cherish our pain, to wear it thin like a child's favorite security blanket. In this way we remain mired in distress, unable to see better options. Inertia rules.

I have found two energies that have the power to free us from the oppressive weight of that inertia: pain and hope. Sometimes, a situation in our lives hurts so badly that we will try anything that could conceivably relieve the pain. Other times, we have such a bright and glorious vision of what could be (or at least a glimpse of one) that we feel compelled to reach for it. Occasionally we are fortunate to have these two elements come together in an exquisite moment of insight.

In those moments, which can never be planned, we simultaneously push away from our accustomed hurt and rush toward our newborn hope. By letting go in that magical instant between the two, we leap free of our past, and all things are possible.

The Toy Rifle

In a conflict resolution workshop with Turkish Cypriots on the troubled island of Cyprus, I began by asking the usual question, "Why are you here?" One young man shared that his father had been killed by Greek Cypriots in the communal violence when he was a child, and that he had grown up full of hatred and bitterness toward his "enemy."

A few evenings before this meeting, the man had gone in to kiss his young son good-night. As he leaned over to hug the child, he noticed a wooden toy rifle tucked under the sheets beside the boy. "Why do you have that rifle in bed with you?" asked the father. "To kill the Greek Cypriots when they come for me in the night," replied his son matter of factly.

In that moment, something shifted in the father's heart. Seeing the need to break the cycle of violence, the man released his own bitterness and made a commitment to work for a future in which his son would not have to live in fear or repeat the hatreds of yesterday.

Vision at the Checkpoint

When we want to build a house, we hire an architect to help us picture how it will look when complete. Likewise, if we want to build peace in any part of our lives, we need to create a blueprint for how it will be. A blueprint, to be effective, should be both thorough and detailed, covering not only what the finished product will look like but also how it will be built. A blueprint is also imbued with our values. We build our homes based on what is important and meaningful to us.

Each of us can create a peace blueprint in our minds. This vision is the map that tells us how to place one foot in front of another, that shows us the direction and the means to achieve our goal. It allows us to realize our dreams. Without it, we flounder in good intentions or vague stirrings. What, exactly, would we like in our relationship with our life partners, our bosses, our mothers? What are our hopes and dreams for our children? How would we like our city or national government to serve us? If we don't ask the questions, how will we ever find the answers?

Once I was running a workshop for a group of Palestinian educators in the West Bank, just on the border of Jerusalem. Below our window there was an Israeli military checkpoint, at which Palestinian cars entering Jerusalem were stopped for security checks.

In the workshop, we were exploring deep questions of vision and values. What did *peace* mean to the educators? What were the essential elements of peace that were important to them? How would their community benefit from peace education? Suddenly, we heard shots being fired outside.

We rushed to the window. Crowds were gathering, sirens were blaring, ambulances and military vehicles were appearing from many directions. We heard that a Palestinian man who had apparently been trying to avoid the checkpoint had been killed by the soldiers, and that another man with him had fled.

What had really happened? Who had been hurt? Who had escaped? Were these relatives of any of our participants? When these and other immediate questions had been answered, we considered what to do next. Should we stop the workshop? Should the participants join their friends and colleagues in the crowd below? How could I possibly ask them to continue to speak about such ephemeral values when on the streets outside there was a very real and compelling crisis?

My Palestinian friends decided the issue. "Out there," they said, pointing to the scene below, "that's our daily reality. In here, we are trying to create something new, something better. This is what's most important. Let's complete the workshop." So we did.

Know Where You Stand

Whether we are talking about motivation, vision, or values, we are dealing with self-knowledge. We need to know who we are and what's important to us before we can reach out to meet another. We must first be grounded in our own reality, and have access to that wisdom by which we come to understand our own nature and circumstances more fully. Knowing where we stand allows us to move from our center with integrity, into any situation that might challenge us.

Cathy Hoffman, Director of the Cambridge Peace Commission in

Cambridge, Massachusetts, tells of an occasion in which young people learned this important lesson.

— The Youth Peace and Justice Corps is a multiracial, multiethnic group of public high school students facilitated by college interns and community activists. The group meets weekly to deal with issues of identity, oppression, the roots of violence, and ways to build community.

In 1998, we were addressing the issue of class on a weekend retreat. A former staff person led us through an exercise designed to identify class background. He asked the group a series of questions, and according to the answer, you either took a step forward or backward: "Step forward if a parent or guardian graduated from college. Take two steps forward if a grandparent graduated from college. Take two steps forward if you expect to get inherited wealth from your parents; one step back if your family expects support from you." After the questions, we created three groups of people, based on the clusters that emerged from these questions: a wealthy group, a middle-class group, and a poor/working-class group.

I went with seven of the students into the wealthy group. "I don't belong here; we don't have any money." "I shouldn't be here; I'm not rich." "As a person of color, I don't belong in this group because I face a lot of discrimination." "My family used to have money but they lost it so I shouldn't be here." There were some of the refrains that opened the circle.

I sat with the tension and then asked, "I wonder if you could think of any ways in which you have resources which might give you advantages over your friends." I was met with silence and some protests that they were not really different from friends. One person talked about her family owning their home and not having any worries about getting into college. I asked again, "I wonder if anyone can think of resources that they have that have nothing to do with money but are related to class."

"Well, my mother is a college dean and when I apply to colleges, she has contacts at other schools. Is that what you mean?" asked one participant. Another said, "Because my parents went to college, they automatically expect I will too. I also know that being at college will be a comfortable place for me. Is that what you mean?" Yet another said, "Even though we don't have any money, my father is very respected for his advanced degrees. I notice that people assume a respect for me and think I'm smart because of him. Is that what you mean?"

Gradually the group came up with a list of dozens of ways in which their class background opened doors or created access that differentiated them from middle-class or poorer friends. Once we broke through the denial and grounded ourselves in our realities, we were ready to go back and talk with others across the class divide.

The Myth of Violence

This story speaks about how honest self-knowledge can motivate us toward peace. One very important piece of self-knowledge concerns the views we hold about violence, at the individual and collective levels.

Many people believe that we are aggressive and violent by nature, and that we have to struggle against this tendency in order to be "civilized." This way of thinking holds that there will always be wars because of our aggressive nature, and that therefore our duty is to be stronger than others so that we can win the inevitable wars. It is a short distance from this thought to the belief that "Might makes right," which affirms the right of the powerful to conquer and dominate the weaker. Certainly this view is driving much of what is happening in our world today, and in the streets of some of our cities.

I hold a different view. I believe that while violence as a way of solving problems is a part of our human repertoire, it is a crude and ultimately ineffective way of getting what we want. I see violence as a learned response to the frustration of our basic human needs—for love and acknowledgment, for safety and security, for belonging and growth—and believe that it flourishes in those times when we are stuck in the mind of separation, when we feel ourselves as individuals without remembering our inherent connection with the wholeness—when we are the drop of water imagining ourselves separate from the ocean.

When entire cultures are operating in the separative mode, the opportunities for learning violence proliferate, because they are socially endorsed. We forget that we have other choices, and we see violence as "how things are." We glamorize violence, as we have today in the United States through our entertainment and news media. Rambo becomes a cultural icon; schoolchildren carry guns to school and mow down their classmates, just like their heroes in the movies; and newspapers report the gory details of every violent crime they can discover, as if only violence is real news.

Tapping the Source of Peace

Other societies glamorize violence in other ways. In extremist groups of several of the world's major religions, violence against the enemy is seen as a righteous act of God's justice, and young men and women are encouraged to give their lives to this cause, being assured that to do so will guarantee reward in the hereafter. In many places of ethnic, communal, or tribal conflict, young children are kidnapped and indoctrinated into a local militia's code of violence, required to prove their worthiness by committing heinous deeds against their own relatives.

I can understand the glamour of violence. Violence provides an adrenaline rush. Whether participating in violence as a spectator or as a perpetrator, that rush can be exciting, compelling, or thrilling, even as it may also be totally terrifying. Literally, the body becomes charged up. When we have experienced this excitement, we may want to repeat it again and again, until it becomes habitual, and we can, in fact, no longer imagine another way.

If we are spectators only, and experience no direct painful effect of the violence, such as through watching television, continuing to witness such activity may be a form of self-pleasuring. If we are violent aggressors, such acts may be a way of announcing our potency. Since violence begets violence, being on the receiving end of violence may simply reinforce our desire to turn around and inflict it on others. We cause pain because we feel pain. Sometimes, even pain can feel good, when it is one of the few ways we have of knowing we are alive.

Breaking the cycle of violence, then, means tearing down the myths that we have built around it, and finding other ways of feeling alive. It also means reestablishing our connection with the Spirit of Peace. The superheroes of nonviolence in our times—Mahatma Gandhi, Martin

Luther King, Jr., and His Holiness the Dalai Lama—have chosen that path from a place of deep spiritual affirmation. They have known the truth of basic unity, and with that knowledge they and their followers have had the moral fortitude to stand calmly in the face of the rage hurled against them, and by doing so, to call those systems of aggression to the transformation point.

We don't all have to be superheroes to choose peace in our lives. When we stand in the experience of our oneness, violence becomes nearly impossible, for hurting another is like hurting ourselves. This truth is the antidote to the myth of violence that is so poisoning our collective life.

Finding the Warrior Within

We each need to discover our own relationship to violence. Even if we hold a strong moral or ethical view about the importance of nonviolence, we need to come to terms with our own experiences of frustration and rage that can turn into violent action. I discovered this for myself through an intense and difficult process.

Some years after healing from cancer, I returned to my home town of Washington, D.C., to care for my invalid parents. I never thought I would live in Washington again; certainly I never cared for the city. Being in the power center of the world was a burden for me, because I could feel the distortions and abuse of power in the very atmosphere around me.

However, there I was, facing a long process of attending to my parents, both of whom had degenerative diseases that would take their lives slowly, year by year. Once I established the routine of their care in our home, I meditated on the next step in my professional life. I had spent many happy years in the mountains of Vermont, far from the political scene, working with people in many capacities, always seeking to grow healthier systems. Should I continue that work in Washington, or was it time for a new expression of service?

The answer that came was shocking to me. "It's time," I heard from deep within, "to take what you know about healing at the individual, family, group, organizational, and community levels to the international arena. It's time to bring the lessons of peace to places of ethnic conflict."

This guidance was hard to accept. Who, me? Work internationally? In places of war? I had three university degrees, but I had deliberately never taken a course in International Relations or Political Science, or anything even remotely related to issues of war and peace. I hardly even read the newspapers, preferring to avoid that helpless feeling that came with hearing about war-induced famine, oppressive totalitarian regimes, nuclear threats, and other such unpleasant topics. Now I was to place myself in the midst of these violent situations, and seek to bring sanity and peace? It was beyond imagining!

I realized that I needed to prepare myself for this challenging task. The preparation took several forms, one of which was to deal with my own strong aversion to violence. I understood that if I were to work in war zones, I would be exposed to a level of violence previously unknown in my life, and to the people who were both perpetrators and victims of that violence. I would likely face soldiers with weapons, and sometimes those weapons might be pointed at me! Me, who avoided conflicts at all costs, and wanted to run when anyone even raised their voice—I would have to stand in the midst of fighting, and offer myself as guide and witness to a better way.

To do this, I realized, I would need to operate in such a setting without reacting—without immediately judging the participants or shrinking from the reality and totality of their experience. I could not afford to let my own revulsion get in the way of understanding the dynamics of the conflict, and its effect on all the parties, including the ones holding the weapons.

In order to deal with this aversion to violence, I decided to psychologically desensitize myself. I spent a year going to every war movie I could find, and reading stacks of soldiers' memoirs and true-life accounts of wartime adventures. I didn't limit myself only to the tales of soldiers. I also read about the experiences of doctors and nurses, bystanders and victims, leaders and followers.

At first I would have to leave the theater in the middle of the film or close the book partway through. Gradually, I was able to stay to the end, without running away. I began to come to terms with the experience of violence, and the profound damage it does to all the parties involved.

There came a time when I noticed a slight shift over some invisible boundary, when I started to feel inside myself the thrill of the kill that was portrayed in these books and movies. It was subtle at first, but eventually I had to admit that I was having a visceral experience of what people called bloodlust. I could understand the rush, the heightened state that some soldiers described, as they poured the power of destruction onto the "enemy."

I could also experience the fear of the firefight, the terror of the trenches or the night patrol, the horror of seeing your friends blown apart beside you, and how that horror could be translated into unthinking brutality against fellow human beings. At the same time, I came to relate to the desire and willingness to live through this kind of nightmare for a greater good—the intention to serve and protect people. When I came to know in myself this range of emotions and possibilities, I met the warrior within, with all her potential for violence and for service, and I was humbled.

What grew in that strange year, with the juxtaposition of offering loving care to my failing parents while simultaneously immersing myself in horrific war stories, was a view of both the particle and the wave. As the particle, I found myself capable, given the right circumstances, of being just as vicious as the most bloodthirsty killer. As the wave, I understood the nature of human suffering when we stray so far from the Spirit of Peace.

Overall, the result was the birth of deep compassion in me, for all of us who cause hurt to, and have been hurt by, one another. Armed only with this compassion, I felt ready to take my place as a peacebuilder in places of deep-rooted conflict around the world.

Let Peace Begin with Me

All of us are peacebuilders in our own lives. We are all called to face and transcend our inclinations to violence, and to break our hearts open to compassion's boundless flow. A first step toward this is the experience of inner peace.

When inner peace is the center from which our lives unfold, we create a wondrous web of love and joy around ourselves. I have often been told that my greatest contribution in situations of hostility or open conflict has been less anything I did or said and more my simple presence in a state of deep inner peace. When we sound that note of inner peace, others around us resonate with it, and can use that resonance to move difficult situations into a new dynamic.

Inner peace comes by following three paths. The first is to make peace *with* ourselves—all of our selves. The second is to make peace *in* ourselves with the significant people in our lives. The third is to find *our own* experience of Peace with a capital P.

There are many ways we fight with ourselves. We believe that we are too much this or not enough that. We isolate aspects of our personalities or our bodies that we wish were different, like our laziness or our fat hips, and do combat with them. We judge ourselves against some internal standard, and come up lacking. We point the finger at our weaknesses, blaming our failings for our unhappiness. We harass ourselves by making, and then promptly breaking, promises to be different.

We will exercise—starting tomorrow! We will diet—but we must have just this one piece of chocolate. If only we weren't so timid (or brash, or ugly, or insensitive, or whatever), we would be living happily ever after right now, with the love of our lives.

Like communities at war, we have our inner factions who struggle against each other, internal polarities that need to find some type of synthesis. Our internal judges collude with our internal victims to assure our continuous punishment for high crimes and misdemeanors; our inner bullies push our inner wimps around the playground of our lives; our interior royalty struggles against our interior commoners for pride of place; our inner consumers clash with our inner environmentalists about that gas-guzzling car we want to buy.

Tapping the Source of Peace

When we enter a new relationship, the part of us that is afraid to love fights with the part of us that craves love. That aspect of us that is afraid of change conflicts with that aspect of us that would venture out into new territory when faced with an opportunity for growth. In short, we continually have interior conflicts between different facets of our own being, and need to find some way of harmonizing the various views.

Finding our inner mediator, and allowing it to do its job, is a lifetime process. We all have different ways of working with ourselves. The important thing is that we be aware of our various subpersonalities, and pay attention to their interactions, many of which are subconscious. We can change the nature of the dialogue, which, if unattended, often becomes fixed in routine and seemingly intractable patterns.

It can be useful to recall that my life is a drama in which I am simultaneously the playwright, the director, the producer, the set designer, the lighting manager, the audience, the actors, and all the characters. Acknowledging all these roles frees me from being a helpless victim of the melodrama of my life, and allows me to be proactive in choosing how my story progresses.

Making peace with ourselves, then, is a process of accepting our multiple voices as an opportunity to determine how we wish to be in any moment. I think I'll interrupt the Judge, whose chastising monologue is getting wearisome. Perhaps I'll allow the Adventurer to explore this new possibility, stretching the safety zone a little further than usual. Maybe I should listen more to what the Wimp needs to feel safe. By what standards have I assumed my hips are too big, and who really cares anyway? If we know we are writing our own stories, we can rewrite them however we choose, to make peace *with* ourselves.

Making peace *in* ourselves with those around us requires the under-standing that responsibility for our relationships is not a 50–50 split, but rather 100 percent for each party in the relationship. That no matter how someone else behaves toward us, what we think and feel about that person and their behavior is under our control, not theirs. If some-one treats me in a way that my feelings are hurt, it is common to say, "You hurt my feelings." The reality, however, is that the behavior may have been unconsciously insensitive or consciously hurtful, but I have a whole range of responses at my disposal. I might feel pain or anger, vengeful or indifferent. I might think you are cruel, ignorant, or silly. These choices are mine, and they are indeed choices, though we usu-ally react so automatically that we forget we do actually make decisions about our feelings.

We've all experienced hurt; we've all had experiences with our loved ones in which our expectations were not fulfilled, our needs were not met, our trust was destroyed, our hearts were broken. What we do with these wounds has a huge impact on our states of inner peace. I'm always struck by those letters in "Dear Abby" from people who haven't spoken to their brothers or mothers in thirty years because of some slight or another. Holding grudges, nurturing the hurt, endlessly going over what we should have said or done, planning our revenge—these are activities that strip away any chance of inner peace, especially when we hold on to the pain from things that hap-pened many years before.

My mother used to say, "Never go to bed angry." In my work as spiritual counselor to people who are dying, I find the same wisdom useful. Finishing our unresolved business with important people in our lives frees us to find that place of inner peace, and we don't have to wait until we are at the edge of death to do it. Indeed, I've found that clearing the air every day, at least in my own heart, is a good mental health practice.

We tend to think we can't resolve these hurts alone, assuming that the other party needs to do or say something that will make it all better. I think otherwise. If I am 100 percent responsible for my part of the relationship, then I can, literally, change my mind about the interaction at any time. In fact, it may be more useful for me to do my internal work alone before I try to explore something different with the other person.

42

The moment when this transformation happens, when we stop looking outward for the solution, and instead focus in, is a profound one. Peacebuilder Jenny McMillan had just this experience with her mother.

My mother is the typical "raised in the Depression" type woman who saves everything and advises everyone to do the same. She shops at Goodwill although she lives in a large home in an expensive neighborhood. If I hear her tell me to save one more time I'd choke her! She was always giving advice and slyly manipulating my life as a teen so that it would turn out the proper, safe way. There was no room for anything entrepreneurial. I must be highly educated in order to get a good job, and it must be in a secure field—the high-paying fields of lawyer, doctor, or engineer.

She was distressed that I didn't marry a highly educated man who would provide properly for the family. She overtly cringed at the liability I assumed in my new business. Most every conversation with her included the word *survival*.

She drove me nuts! I could only hold in my anger at her every suggestion, and I could barely keep my mouth shut at her continuous insinuation that I was not keeping my affairs in proper order.

At least that's the conversation I was having with myself. My mother appeared to me as a nag who had no more insight into what drove her in life than a child.

Then one day as I was standing at the kitchen window, peering out across the farm after hours of handling my own kids and their homework, I realized my experience of my mother was all made up! How I thought of her was merely my interpretation of all she did. In a flash of light I saw that who my mother really is, is a person committed to the well-being and happiness of her children. There has never been an action that she has taken that has not been out of loving concern. Yes, her vision of what was necessary to occur was distorted by her experiences, but the motivation was love. The blinding illusion of my conversation with myself about who my mother is had never let me see this before.

Now, my experience of her is totally transformed. I recognize that my experience is a product of my own mental creation. Now, in those moments of irritation with her, I can recreate my interpretation of her such that I am left with the sense of being loved, and with the sense that she is one of the greatest moms in the world.

Since that time I have come to realize that I have an interpretation of everyone for which I am responsible. With that awareness in mind, I have started to make up empowering interpretations of others, and notice that I am left with the experience of how great people are, which allows me to interact with others in a much different way than ever before!

Tapping the Source of Peace

Jenny's story illustrates our ability to find peace in ourselves concerning relationships with our family when we choose to look at the situation differently.

Healing Our Wounds with God

Another area where many of us are wounded and need to find peace is in our relationships with God or Spirit. All of us are born, I believe, with an inherent knowledge of our divine birthright. Somewhere along the way, however, we may have experiences that leave us deeply disappointed or wounded in our souls.

For some, this pain may arise from a punitive religious view that taught us how "bad" we are. For others, it may be an emptiness that organized religion failed to fill. We may feel a sense of betrayal by a respected spiritual leader, or by the hypocrisy of our religious elders, who preach one thing and practice another.

Perhaps we experienced a terrible loss or suffered horrendous harm, and wondered how any Divine Being could allow such an evil, awful thing to happen. Maybe our faith just slipped away over the years, without our noticing. Then again, it may be that we never really addressed ourselves to the basic question of our spiritual relationship to life, and have no sense of that connection at all.

For myself, this wounding happened during adolescence, when I realized that nothing in my Jewish religious training or experience, in synagogue or at home, was really touching my soul. I felt empty and bitter, and went through a long period of agnosticism. It is true that the near-death event I've described earlier did provide for a profound spiritual awakening, and an ensuing rich spiritual life in the Native American and Tibetan Buddhist traditions. However, it was not until recently, when I discovered a form of Jewish practice and celebration that finally addressed my spiritual nature and got those holy juices flowing, that my original soul wound was finally healed.

However it happens, our split from Spirit is damaging to our very core, and there can be no real inner peace until we somehow mend this relationship. Obviously, our spiritual journey unfolds over the whole of our lifetime, and is not about a single moment or episode. Nonetheless, I have discovered that inner peace is fundamentally a state of spiritual connection, and if that connection is flawed or marred by an overlay of anger, grief, or distrust, the circuit cannot be completed.

The Energy of Peace

In order to vibrate with the energy of peace, we need to plug in directly to the Source. This vibration is unique. It is distinguishable from, though closely related to, the signature of love, beauty, or any other of the great ideals, just as the timbre of a trombone is different from, though similar to, that of trumpet or French horn.

Once we've known this energy of peace fully, in every atom of our being, we can use various devices to help us remember how to come home again. Like home base in a baseball game, this becomes the place we start from and return to, in our run around the bases of life.

We all have different doorways to this home base. Some of us work best through imagery, others through metaphor, still others through sound or words, or through movement or a direct bodily experience. If

I can recall a moment in my life, or a place in my life, where I felt that deep "peace that passeth understanding," I can anchor that memory in my visual and cellular screen, and come home to it whenever I choose.

One way I get there is through images of being in the natural world. I see myself on the beach, hearing the waves crash and swirl along the shore, and feeling the hot dry sand between my toes. Sometimes I picture myself sitting on a cliff, with my back against a pine tree, looking out over a sparkling lake, with the wind brushing my face. Other times I think of sitting by a fire at night, watching the sparks showering up into the darkness, or resting on the rocks in a canyon, beside a rushing brook, in the chill twilight air.

I also find certain mundane life activities can take me home to peace. Ironing or balancing my checkbook work for me, I think because they are about putting things in order and seeing everything come out right. Whatever avenue we use, once we can identify the particular vibration of peace that these experiences engender, we can tune our antennae to this frequency and find that channel again and again. And finding that channel allows us to broadcast from the peace station, in any situation, from the inside out.

Resting in the Stillness

One element of this vibration of peace has to do with what I call "the serenity stream." This is the aspect of peace that is about calm, order, and tranquility. It is the place where the vast stillness lies, a stillness that replenishes us infinitely.

We are busy people, with busy minds. Our external stimulation and internal chatter are endless. We can distract ourselves briefly by watching television, reading a magazine or book—anything to engage our mind with someone else's story—but ultimately we come again and again to weaving our own story in our minds. To get beneath this layer of mental activity is not easy, yet that is the path that reaches beyond confusion into quietude.

"I just want some peace and quiet around here," we say, linking the two. We know instinctively that to have access to our deepest resources, we need to find ways to silence the noise in our heads and the tension in our bodies, and to relax. Just as the surface of the ocean is churned into waves by the wind, so are our minds agitated by ceaseless currents of thought. Yet beneath the waves of both ocean and mind lies a deep stillness. The quiet of peace is to be found in that stillness.

How to stop the flow of mind and the activity of the body long enough to drop into that quietude is a subject addressed by the various meditation traditions of the world. Some of those systems are quite elaborate; others are unbelievably simple. No matter how we do it, we all need to surrender to the deep silent harmony that is at the core of our being on a regular basis. We need to relax into it, let our everyday realities slip away for a short time, and allow ourselves to rest in that infinite serenity.

This is the place beyond doing, where we simply are. This is the place where, as the tension drains out, the restorative flow of the life force washes gently through every atom of our being. This is the place from which all things arise, and to which all things return. This is the home of the Spirit of Peace, the wellspring of true power—the power to be all that we truly are, the divine One that we are.

We can find this stillness with outer help—by going to places of beauty, by having a massage, by listening to music—or through inner means—by meditation, conscious relaxation, or breath work. The path is not so important. What's important is that we find a way that works for us to get there, so that we can rest in the stillness. Without rest, no life form can thrive and grow. We need quiet time so that we can both discharge the tensions we carry, and recharge with inspiration and renewal. We also need that quiet time for listening. For it is only in the stillness that the voice of our highest self, the Spirit of Peace, can be heard, leading us to action that will translate that primordial harmony into the comings and goings of our daily lives.

From Inner Peace to Outer Peace

Peace around us and peace within us are intimately related to one another. If our surroundings are serene, it reminds us to get quiet and relax. If we are at peace within ourselves, it radiates to those around us, and literally changes the vibration of the circumstances or interaction.

Janet Kahn, a peace educator from Silver Spring, Maryland, tells of such a time.

In the fall of 1994 I had the honor of spending one day every few weeks studying peace with a classroom of nine- to twelve-year-olds at the Children's Montessori School in Ipswich, Massachusetts. When I entered the classroom on the first day, my intention was to share much of what I had learned from studying the Cherokee tradition of Peace Villages. My plans changed, however, almost immediately.

In that first discussion, which was on the meaning of peace, I noticed the students seemed to have difficulty listening to one another. They interrupted each other. They rarely really looked at the speaker. Sometimes they seemed so intent on what they wanted to say next that they couldn't really hear what the speaker was saying. Perhaps they feared it would bump their own ideas out of their minds. Since these conditions were interfering with our personal peace, and because they certainly were interfering with good relations in the classroom, listening became the subject of inquiry in our study of peace.

To begin, we each identified one or two people to whom we most enjoyed talking when we had something important to share. Then we described to each other how it feels to talk to that person, and why he or she is the one to whom we would want to bring our thoughts, concerns, excitements.

We realized that all of us were identifying pretty much the same quality in these especially good listeners. We were saying that when we talk with these people, they give us their undivided attention, and that means the world to us. They don't listen to us and make dinner or talk on the phone at the same time. They don't interrupt us and make their ideas the center of the discussion. They don't listen to us and think about how we could have done things better. When we are talking to these good listeners about something important, they look at us and respect us with their full attention.

Having discovered the key to good listening, the kids were then anxious to practice it. On the surface it seemed pretty simple, because they only had to do one thing at a time—listen. They gave it a go, launching into their next discussion determined to really listen to one another. They certainly did better than when they hadn't been concentrating on it. Yet they could see that there was more to this "one thing at a time" business than they had initially understood.

I confessed that doing one thing at a time was actually a somewhat rare and special event for me. Just that morning, for instance, on my way to school, I had been simultaneously driving the car, eating a bagel, listening to the radio, and imagining how things might go in the classroom that day. I also told them that, as easy as it might sound to just do one thing at a time, people actually spend years practicing it. I told them that this is what meditation is all about: quieting the mind and learning to bring your complete attention to one thing at a time. We decided to meditate together at the beginning of each of our classes, hoping it would help our discussions.

In the following weeks we tried a number of methods for quieting our minds. We did guided visualizations; we followed our breath; we listened to a tone and followed it into silence. We also used some of Vietnamese Buddhist monk Thich Nhat Hanh's methods, saying, for instance, on every in-breath, "I am aware that I am breathing in," and on the out-breath, "I am aware that I am breathing out," or "Breathing in, I know that now is the only moment. Breathing out, I know this is a wonderful moment." At the end of each meditation session, the students had the opportunity to share anything they wanted about their experiences. We talked about all the things meditators notice: how much our minds like to yack at us; how our rear end feels when we are just sitting on it moment after moment with nothing taking our attention away from that sensation; how easily we are distracted by the people around us; all the reasons we wanted to open our eyes at various moments (nervousness, curiosity).

Then, one day, while we were meditating, the room suddenly got incredibly quiet. It wasn't just a no-sound kind of quiet; it was something else. Checking in with each other later, we realized that this kind of quiet felt really good to a lot of us. Then someone mentioned that part of the quietness was that for some reason, all of the animals in the room had gotten quiet with us. This classroom included a number of animals. There was Grateful the rat, a half dozen or so gerbils, a cockatiel, and various other critters.

We hadn't realized it, but usually when we were meditating, in the background we could hear the scratching of the rodents, the whirring of the gerbils' equipment, a call or fluttering from the bird. On this day, we realized that we had created together a peace so palpable that every life form in the room had responded to it by joining us. Everyone had gotten calm. In that way, the animals helped us understand the meaning, and the power, of that deep stillness we experienced as peace.

This vibrational impact of inner peace that Janet is talking about can hold us in good stead as we meet the difficulties of life. It once even prevented a difficult situation in my life from turning dangerous. I was passing through a military checkpoint late at night. It was during a period of high tension and sporadic outbursts in a country racked by decades of recurring violence. I had been filming interviews with prominent intellectuals from the faction seen by the government as rebels or terrorists. At that time, individuals from that faction who cooperated with foreign media were often placed in detention by government authorities.

The filming had gone surprisingly well, especially considering the logistical and security challenges of bringing a camera into a military setting, where armed soldiers roamed the streets and the slightest uncommon event could set in motion a full-fledged street riot, or worse.

The film I was making was not partisan. I had interviewed people from both sides equally, seeking to find and to show common ground and a shared desire for peace. But on this night, as I was returning to the capital city from deep in "enemy" territory, the relief and excitement of having accomplished a difficult and scary task made me blind to the dangers still present in the situation. I lost my concentration, and in the process, put many people at risk.

When I packed the car after the filming session, I neglected to put the big, studio-sized video camera in the car's trunk, where it could be covered with boxes and clothes, out of immediate sight. Instead, I placed it casually on the back seat of the car next to me. It was only as we approached the midnight checkpoint that I remembered the extent to which the presence of such a camera could create trouble for my evening's hosts, who had put their own safety at stake to cooperate with my project.

I had the briefest of moments to prepare myself. Physically I reacted by placing the folds of my skirt over the camera, knowing full well that this would be futile in the likely event that the soldiers asked everyone in the car to get out. Emotionally, I tuned in to the courage and kindness of my hosts, who had so willingly risked their safety for the opportunity to speak a message of peace. I knew I could never betray them.

At the same time, I tuned in to the soldiers manning the outpost. Their highest goal, too, came from a place of internal logic and integrity. Their mission was to protect the people in the city, and to screen the possible import of anything or anyone that could fuel the fires of violence already burning so close to the surface.

Holding that thought of the dignity of both sides, I slipped into a place I have learned to go when things get difficult. I opened my heart to the flow of love and appreciation for all in this conflict who were struggling to find a better way. I saw the soldiers as whole and holy beings, doing the best they could to care for their people. I saw my hosts as whole and holy beings, doing the best they could to care for their people. I called on the Spirit of Peace, and filled the car with her light.

As we drove up to the soldier at the gate, I simply sat and radiated that light. The soldier began to question the driver sternly, while he looked inside the car, sweeping into its corners with his watchful eyes. When he saw me, something softened. He straightened, smiled, and waved us through.

Remembering Our Wholeness

Becky's story brings many of these elements of peace together in one place. She was a sickly young woman in her early twenties when I met her. She had had severe liver disease since early childhood, and each year her doctors had told the family that it could well be her last.

Becky came to me seeking spiritual counsel and healing. She was determined to live fully in whatever time she had. She was not attempting necessarily to cure her liver disease, as the physical deterioration was profound. She did wish, though, for a better quality and richness of life.

One of the things Becky most wanted to experience was motherhood. She had been told she could not survive pregnancy, and indeed it was a moot point, because Becky never had had regular menstrual periods.

In our first session together, Becky went into a deep meditation, during which she saw deeply into the atomic structure of her cells, and also out into the farthest galaxies of space, and recognized that they were different expressions of the same pattern. When she came out of the meditation, she ecstatically announced a realization both simple and profound: "I am a part of all that is!" With this new awareness, Becky went home and shortly thereafter began to have her periods.

At a subsequent session, Becky did another meditation, in which she imagined her liver in its ideal form: healthy and vital, strong and fully functioning. She drew a picture of this ideal liver, and put it up over her bed. Every morning she would look at the picture and affirm, "I am a healthy liver." Not long after this, Becky got pregnant.

Defying all medical odds and predictions, Becky went on to deliver a healthy baby boy and, though she went through many ups and downs, was able to enjoy her precious son for his first three years. She died peacefully, surrounded by friends and family, long after her liver could, by medical standards, still be functioning. But Becky was living on a different kind of medicine. Remembering herself as one with all that is, and as a healthy liver, were her tonics for inner peace and survival.

Recalling our sacred wholeness, as Becky was able to do, is the first concrete and practical step we can take toward creating peace in our lives—whether we seek to stop beating ourselves up, get along better with our mates, or find a way to bring more peace into the wider world. When connected with that primal remembrance, even briefly, we are able to access our will, our vision, our ideals and values, our motivation, our higher purpose, our higher power, and that essential vibration of Peace, all of which are critical tools of peacemaking.

These tools are like trampolines. They allow us to jump high, beyond our normal, limited vision of everyday reality. Without access to these, our lives are like wheels spinning deeper and deeper into muddy ruts. With access, we find the energy to break through impasses, to transform obstructions, even to break our addictions or invite miracles.

Tapping the Source of Peace: Centering Home

I call this ability to remember our wholeness and drop into the vibration of peace "centering home," a phrase I've drawn from a song title written by my dear friend Molly Scott. By "centering home," I mean touching the Source within myself. This is a skill that, like any other, is acquired through practice. I'm going to offer it here to you because I happen to believe that this is the single most important skill for being a peacemaker.

Most people, when faced with a conflict or a problem, want to move immediately to action or problem-solving mode, and "fix" it. When we do this, however, we are acting from only a small part of the resources available to us, and we may actually make the problem grow larger.

If, instead, we take the time to ground ourselves in that home base of inner peace, we have gained in three ways. First, we have a better understanding of what's really important to us. Second, by connecting with our own wholeness and our oneness with all that is, we are rooted in our integrity, and can move in any direction, as needed, from the totality of our being. Finally, by being plugged into this power, we have access to far more information and energy than if we react from a place of imbalance.

Centering home for me is like dropping into the right slot. There is a glorious sense of "Ahhhh," as if everything has just slipped into perfect alignment. There is a sense of effortlessness, while at the same time a great vitality and dynamism.

Many years ago, before I began meditating, I remember asking a friend who was then involved with Buddhist meditation, "What do you actually do there on the cushion while you're meditating?" She replied that her instructions were to pay attention to her breathing, watching the in-breath and the out-breath. When her mind wandered off to everyday concerns, or to anything other than simple awareness of the breath, she was to say, "Thinking," and gently, without judgment, bring the mind back to the breath.

As a metaphor, that was a major life lesson for me. Anyone who is not a master at meditation would certainly not be able to be 100 percent attentive to the breath. What matters is not that we be in that groove constantly, but that, when we find we have wandered from it, as we inevitably will, we gently bring our awareness back.

So it is with centering home. I am not always there, in that place of deep inner peace. I have personally not met anyone who is. The path of spiritual evolution is the ability increasingly to remember our true nature and to be able to return there faster and faster. This takes great practice.

There are multiple dimensions to centering home. We can do it physically, mentally, emotionally, and spiritually. When all aspects are aligned, the "Ahhhh" is especially satisfying.

There are many pathways, and they are all ways of transcending our everyday minds, our single water-drop identities, and becoming one with the universal Mind, or the vast ocean. One pathway is through vision—our hopes and dreams. When we see our highest ideal of how we want to be in any given situation, that helps us center home. Another is through acknowledging our values. Those qualities that we cherish, that give meaning to our life, these can carry us home. When we are motivated to peace through vision and values, we are connected to our higher selves, and the power of that carries us along.

Likewise, tapping into our intention, as I did in choosing to live fully and joyously, can be a major route back home. Aligning our personal wills with the larger Divine Will—the will to be in harmony and peace with our friends and relations—is a critical step to knowing deep peace, for then we can relax into that "Ahhhh" and act from a conscious place of purpose and commitment.

Finally, through creativity we can center home, opening our mind to the flow of information and possibility that surrounds us always, on many levels. The connection allows our intuition to flourish, and makes synergy more likely, thus making a clearer path to that which needs resolution and transformation.

Whatever path we take, the practice of centering home brings us to a direct knowledge of the energy of peace. We can use that energy to bathe in the flow of serenity, renewing ourselves in the tranquil pool of inner peace. Or we can use it to reach out in action, carrying that vibration directly into our relationships with friends and family, neighbors and colleagues.

Tapping the Source of Peace

When we do this, we are living with hope. I often work in places of deep-rooted conflict, with people who have experienced immeasurable suffering. They feel weighted down by despair, and do not see how their situations can improve. I used to come away from these occasions feeling sad and helpless, wondering if anything that I had done, or could do, would possibly make a difference.

I discovered, however, that some other, quieter, magic is at work on a more subtle level in these circumstances. People report to me that the very fact of my presence and caring, and my ability to radiate inner peace in a situation of heightened conflict and tension act like beacons of hope.

This hope is the antidote to the poisons of chronic despair. It keeps us going through the unspeakable darkness of the cruelty and violence we do to one another in the name of our cherished causes. It is the doorway to that better way we are seeking. We have heard many stories of people imprisoned and tortured by repressive regimes, who were able to survive because they knew that someone on the outside was keeping hope alive for their release.

Hope is powerful because it is the spark of the life force that refuses to die. It reminds us that the Spirit of Peace exists, even when we can't see it or touch it. Hope is the key. Without hope, we stop breathing, we stop trying. With hope, even when it is held by someone else, we take the next breath, and the next, and reach gently into the realm of possibility. When we remember, even if as in a dream, that peace is truly possible, then it is. Truly possible. When we find the hope of peace, we have begun the journey at its source.

Practice Centering Home

Here are some ways you can practice accessing your endless source of inner peace, bringing forth ideals and values that you can concretely apply in your immediate life.

1. *Meditative Practice for Centering Home*

Sit quietly in a place that feels comfortable and safe for you. Put your feet flat on the floor, hands in your lap. You may want to close your eyes, though it isn't necessary. Let your spine be gently erect without effort. Relax your shoulders. Let your head find its natural center over your spine. Reach your energy up through the top of your head as if to the sky above, and at the same time release all physical tension, as if your spine were suspended from above, falling naturally into perfect alignment. At the same time, be aware of your feet on the ground, and your seat upon the chair or cushion. You are connected to both earth and sky. Breathe easily and allow the body to gently adjust itself to this state of alignment. This is center, home base. How do you feel?

Now try leaning side to side, forward and back, passing through this center point to a place off-balance, always returning to center. Notice the difference between being off-base and being home.

Now bring your attention to your breath. Simply notice the in-breath and the out-breath. Notice the natural cycle and rhythm of your breathing. You don't have to make anything happen. Just watch the circular motion of the in-breath turning to become the out-breath, and the out-breath turning to come in again. On the out-breath, release the body's tension and busyness of mind. On the in-breath, draw in a stream of fresh and revitalizing life force. How do you feel?

Go back and check your spine again, and come back to center as you need to. Put the sitting center and the breathing center together, being aware of both simultaneously, and notice how you feel.

Next, invite the thought of Peace into your mind. Trust whatever comes when you think of Peace: perhaps an image or set of images; perhaps a sensation; perhaps an awareness, an insight, or a memory; perhaps some words. Continue to sit for a moment, conscious of the breath, aligned physically with center, inviting Peace into your consciousness. When you have a clear sense of Peace, breathe into it. Let it fill you from the inside out. What do you notice?

You can stop this practice after a few moments and open your eyes. Look around you. You have just centered home, and tapped into the source of peace. How do you feel? Think of one situation in your life where this experience or the insights arising from it could be usefully applied. How might you do that?

2. Action Practice for Centering Home

Think of a relationship in your life that is not in harmony or that you would like to improve. Take a piece of paper, write the name of the person across the top, and put a line down the middle. Label one side "Ideals" and the other side "Actions."

Ask yourself, "Why is this relationship important to me? What is my vision for the relationship—if it were functioning at its highest expression, what would it look and feel like? What values or qualities would I like to manifest in this relationship?" Then, in the Ideals column, list the qualities, values, images, or phrases that come to you in response to these questions. This column represents your ideals for the relationship.

Now, in the Action column, list some possible and feasible actions you might take to realize those ideals. For instance, let's say you chose your life partner or best friend as the relationship you want to improve. Let's say that in your Ideals column you listed "Trust" and "Playfulness," among other things. For actions, to improve trust, you might decide to share this list with your friend, and talk openly about what trust means to each of you. You might even wish to identify the places where trust has been difficult, and consider what you can each do about it.

To address Playfulness, you might list the option of buying a new board game and inviting your friend or partner to play it with you one evening, or getting a box of outlandish clothes from a thrift shop and inviting a group of people, including your special one, for an evening of dress-up and skits.

Making this list is an important step toward translating your ideals into action, but it is only the first step. The important thing here is not so much the specific action you name, but rather that you can see possibilities for actions that will embody your ideals. Now your task is to make choices about which items in your Actions column you will actually do. Then do them!

TWO

In the mirror, I see only
A reflection of the you in me.
I return the mirror,
To share the gift
Of the me in you.
Now, when I look where the mirror was,
I see our children,
Fruit of our single dream.

Awakening the Mind of Peace

All My Relations

THE PHRASE, "All My Relations," is the English-language rendition of a term used by the Lakota Sioux and other Native American nations to express the understanding that every living being is my relative. It is traditionally spoken as an affirmation of our sacred interrelatedness, and also as a prayer and dedication, that any good produced by my actions might benefit all beings in the web of life.

I came to the truth behind "All My Relations" over a four-year period of healing, after my cancer and near-death experience. As I described, I spent much of that time exploring the natural world, learning the lessons of how to live fully and joyously. What started as almost an intellectual exercise, however, soon became a mind-shattering experience.

I remember, for instance, looking at flowers—flowers in gardens, along dusty roadsides, in the deep shady woods, rimming ponds and marshes. At first I marveled at the variety of shapes, sizes, and colors. Then I noticed the center. Each and every flower, no matter how small or large, had a center. I began to ask how I might be like the flower. Did I have a center? If so, what or where was it? What was the relationship between my center and a flower's center?

I would also examine trees—fruit trees in full blossom, stately oaks, proud pines, graceful birches. I noticed that trees grow in two directions at once—through their roots into the earth, and through their branches and leaves up toward the sun. What were my roots? How did I, like the tree, reach deep into the dark and loamy earth around my roots, seeking and drawing nourishment for my growth? What parts of me stretched up to meet the sun, to dance within the light?

These questions moved beyond the rhetorical as I began to have a direct experience of my center, my roots, and my light-seeking branches. I felt not only a relationship with the flower or tree, but also some subtle communication. The tree was showing me my roots; the flower was telling me about center. I was learning to listen in a new way.

The most important teachers for me soon became the winged ones—those relatives who fly. A red-gold dragonfly visited me one day, resting on my arm. She showed me her shimmering, radiant beauty and, in admiring her, I found my own beauty. Another time a hummingbird entered my home, and couldn't find its way out. As I tried to rescue him, he died in my hands. I was deeply moved. He came to me, and literally gave his life so that I might learn about impermanence.

In one magic moment, all these lessons came together for me as a gift from a flock of birds. It was toward the end of my healing period. I went to Sannibel Island, a beach along the west coast of Florida, to escape the late winter doldrums of Vermont. On Sannibel there is a very special place, the Ding Darling Wildlife Sanctuary, which is a haven for tropical birds of all kinds. I had been to Ding Darling once before, and felt a pull to be there again. I knew I needed to be there at sunset.

I stood at the edge of a pond in the sanctuary just as the sun was hanging on the horizon before me. There, resting on the still water, was a large flock of white ibis—sacred birds in ancient Egypt. All at once, as if they were a single being with one mind, they lifted off the water. As they flew, I flew with them, dipping and gliding on the sunset currents. I could feel us moving together, in a flying dance of holy joy.

Their flight patterns were mirrored on the surface of the pond in the day's dying light, like a mirror to my soul, to our shared spirit. They came low over my head, circling around me, as if anointing me with their feathered blessing, then landed, again in perfect unison, on the water before me.

At that moment I felt impelled to look down at my feet. There, waiting, was a large feather. I extended the feather out toward the sun, and the sun's last rays filtered through the feather to make iridescent rainbows on my arm. In that moment, I remembered my true nature,

Awakening the Mind of Peace

like the sun-feather. The cancer—literally, the tumor, and figuratively, my way of being as I was growing the cancer—had been like a tight fist: impacted, rigid, hard. The healing process had shown me a better way to live—open and free, in a perpetual dance of grace and beauty, flying in the light and resting on the still waters. The flight of the ibis was my final exam and my valedictory, all wrapped up together, and the sun-feather my graduation gift.

The winged ones continue to be my guide through life, showing me new directions, confirming ideas that come to me in wonder, reminding me to center home. Though I often slip back into forgetfulness, they always return, bringing my attention gently back, like the mind returning to the breath, to the remembrance that we are all relatives.

I have discovered, as the Native American cosmology teaches, that this relatedness is not a metaphor but a living power. With all creatures we have a mutual capacity for communication, love, and learning; with all beings we are in a continuous subtle exchange of energy and information. The fact that most of us have forgotten this bond, or feel unskilled with it, does not make it disappear, nor render it irrelevant. On the contrary: we can be encouraged that, by entering the Age of Information, humanity is discovering means by which we can be more plugged in to this network around the world.

Now when I say, "All My Relations!" in prayer or in affirmation, it is those ibis I most honor. They brought me through the doorway of ignorance to the realm of true relationship, in a blessing ceremony more poignant than any manmade ritual I've ever known. I am grateful.

Spiritual Lesson 2:
We Belong to Each Other

I once went to a conference to which Mother Teresa had been invited. Unable to attend, she sent a message to be read to the assembly. One phrase from that message penetrated my heart like an arrow. "We belong to each other," she said.

This sentence puts into words a deep spiritual truth that is a logical consequence of the basic nature of reality as we know it. If we posit the unity of all creation, then it makes sense that within that unity we are all related to one another. Arising from the same Source, we are inevitably connected to each other. Carrying the same sacred essence, we are linked through that essence in a single web of life.

Interconnectedness. Interrelatedness. Interdependence. These words have become popularized in our vocabulary through the growth in recent decades of environmental awareness. We have learned, much to our dismay, that the burning of rain forests in Brazil does indeed impact our global climate, which in turn affects our regional weather, which in turn affects our daily lives. We have discovered that the hydrofluorocarbons we release into the atmosphere from our air conditioners do indeed affect the ozone layer around our planet, which in turn affects our possibility of getting skin cancer, and possibly other diseases as well.

These have been—and still are—hard lessons for humanity to learn. We want to do things that make our lives immediately easier or more profitable; we don't want to think about how it might affect some stranger on the other side of the world in twenty years' time. Yet what better teacher than the natural world to hold up to our eyes, like a mirror, the basic truth of how we are, inexorably and ineradicably, related to one another, in all forms of life?

The growing environmental movement has shown us that every living thing is part of this same fragile web of life on this planet we all call home. We poison the waters with our waste. Fish die. Birds that eat the fish collect toxins in their bodies. Their eggs become brittle, unviable. Whole species decline or become extinct. Animals that rely on those eggs go hungry. They seek alternative food sources, perhaps invading back yards or city streets to find new ways to satisfy their hunger. Other critters, the common prey of those birds, are no longer kept in check, and overpopulate an area. The balance of the food chain is disturbed in every direction.

Meanwhile, because of the same poisoned fish, fishermen can no longer earn a decent living. Communities go into economic decline. Alcoholism increases. Young people move to the cities seeking jobs. Family ties and traditional ways are strained or broken. Alienation increases. And so on.

The natural world is the most obvious teacher about our interrelatedness. It is a bit more of a stretch for us to feel any direct relationship to people in cultures profoundly different from ours. What, after all, does a pigmy in Chad have in common with a stockbroker on Wall Street? What relation could there possibly be between a shepherd on the steppes of Uzbekistan and a sales clerk in a clothing store in Miami Beach? Even within one American city, two teenagers might live in totally different worlds—one in an affluent neighborhood, one in an impoverished public housing project.

Yet the explosion of telecommunications has brought us face to face with our planetary neighbors so sharply that we can experience a war or famine halfway around the world in the comfort of our own living room. Economic and political globalization, along with the means to communicate instantly, have ensured that we know about and feel the direct impact of faraway financial or governmental changes instantly.

At the same time, the movement of large populations, through normal immigration and disaster-induced refugee streams, continues to bring new faces, languages, and traditions into contact with each other, with all the benefits and stresses such pluralism can bring. Meanwhile, we are confronting new scourges that defy simple solutions precisely because they transcend national boundaries. Environmental degradation, drugs, AIDS, money laundering, and terrorism are not limited to the narrow confines of any one nation, but move among and between us all. In fact, the technology for transportation and communication that has allowed for financial globalization now also benefits those who traffic in nefarious goods—drugs, arms, sex—allowing them to hook up vast and dangerous worldwide enterprises for criminal activity.

The late twentieth century will be known, I believe, for this incredible breakdown of local and national boundaries. For whatever good or ill this phenomenon may bring, it shows us the undeniable fact and power of our interconnectedness.

Being connected in this way, we naturally depend on one another for our survival and well-being. If one neighborhood allows toxic waste dumping in a river, the downstream cities will feel the effects. If one school district is particularly successful in preparing its students for the workplace, the benefit from that on local industry may translate into a stronger economy for the whole region.

Depending on one another in this way, both locally and globally, means we are in each others' hands. Our fate rests not on our actions alone, but on the thoughts and deeds of those around us, individually and collectively. And the fate of strangers halfway around the world likewise rests in our hands. Thus Mother Teresa's comment that we belong to each other makes perfect sense. We are in each other's keeping, whether we like it or not.

What Is Right Relationship?

We all have our own ideas about what is right and what is wrong, based on our cultures, values, and personal preferences.

Having said that, I find the Buddhist term "right relationship" compelling, exactly because it calls me to think about what I mean by *right*. In my pursuit of this question, I have found some basic qualities of relationship, or ways that we treat one another, that people across many cultures seem to agree are important.

No matter where we live or what our cultural background, we all want to be treated kindly and with respect. We all want to be dealt with fairly or justly. We want to be acknowledged and appreciated for who we really are. We want to live free of coercion. We want to love and be loved. We want to feel safe. We want to feel included, to belong. We want to feel powerful, that we matter, that we make a difference. We want this for ourselves as individuals, and for the groups we identify with.

However, these words, simple as they appear on paper, do not necessarily connote shared meaning. In late twentieth-century America, for a man to open the door for a woman may feel like respectful behavior to some, condescending or demeaning behavior to others. People who use corporal punishment on their children may believe it is a way of showing love. The child may experience it differently.

This range of opinions may suggest that, like beauty, right relation-ship is in the eye of the beholder, or like art, we know it when we see it. In other words, there is a subjective quality to how we describe right relationship, but we instinctively know when we are being treated in a good way—a way that nourishes us—or not.

With or without a clear definition, if we are treated in ways that feel particularly bad, we might be prepared to fight, to kill, or even to die for the right to be accorded that which we believe we deserve as true human beings. Right relationship is that important.

Quality Counts

We are all relatives in a single family of life on this planet and beyond. This means the giraffe, the dragonfly, the apple tree, the river, and the millipede are all my relatives. The housewife with three little kids down the street from me is my relation, as is the homeless man panhandling on the corner a continent away.

The fact of our relationship is a given; it is not a choice. We are all, and always, in relationship. I cannot choose to be interconnected with one neighbor and not another. I can only choose how I will experi-ence and express that relationship. My choice is always and only about the quality and shape of the relationship, not about its existence.

If my choice is about the quality of relationship, I prefer high qual-ity to low. Why would I want a broken-down jalopy when I could drive a safe, reliable car? Why would I want to drink spoiled milk if I could have fresh? Why would I want an enemy if I could have a friend?

To say I choose high-quality relationship does not mean that I necessarily treat everyone exactly the same. I certainly have a closer relationship with my daughter than with the young woman I pass daily in the parking lot. I surely speak more intimately with a life partner than with the checkout clerk at the grocery store.

The degree of relationship changes, in terms of closeness and intimacy or depth of feeling. The commitment to quality, however, remains the same. I can treat the worm on the sidewalk with as much respect as I treat my best friend. That doesn't mean I share my inner secrets with the worm; it does mean I take care not to step on it.

Suddenly, I arrive at a deceptively familiar place; I arrive at the truth expressed in the Golden Rule. I need to treat people, indeed all beings, with the same quality of respect, fairness, appreciation, and honesty that I wish to receive from them. To "Love your neighbor as yourself" or to "Do unto others as you would have them do unto you" (or however this thought may be expressed in its many cultural and religious variations) is no longer a moral imperative—a "should"—but a natural implication of our interrelatedness. We need to hold and cherish one another with care precisely because we belong to each other. What we give comes back to us. The circle is completed. The one that we are is all of us.

Relationships on Purpose

If we choose the quality of our relationships, then we need some guidelines or yardstick by which to determine what quality we shall aim for. One such guideline has to do with the purpose of the relationship.

I once had a business partner who was married to my best friend. We started our business with all the best intentions. It didn't work out at a personal level between us, though the business was a good one and could have thrived. Soon we were both angry and blaming one another. Going to work became a trial, and my relationship with my best friend began to suffer as well, as she was inevitably put in the middle.

I thought deeply about the ultimate aim of my relationship with this man. Was it more important that we stay in the business and work out our issues with each other? Or was it more important that I let the business go and focus back on my friendship with him and his wife? Since our conflict was solely about running the business, enjoying his presence in social circumstances was not a problem.

I struggled with this question for some time, until it became apparent that the highest good to be gained here was not in the business, but in the friendship. We were able to dissolve the business amicably, and with it the tension and struggle between us.

If I hadn't been able to focus on the purpose of that relationship, I would undoubtedly have stayed in the conflict beyond the point of no return, destroying both the business and the friendship.

When I speak of purpose, I am referring to my highest ideal, or hope and aspiration, for the particular relationship. This is an important distinction. If I am moving a little too slowly in traffic, and the driver behind me suddenly passes me, shouting and gesticulating his road rage as he goes by, I don't have to react angrily. I can silently wish him a good day, because I have no intention for any ongoing relationship with him.

With my best friend's husband, however, I had an ideal I wished to satisfy. I could picture, and desire, a high-quality friendship between his family and mine. The sisterhood I felt with his wife stood like a beacon, calling me to align my actions toward that goal. In this sense, understanding the purpose of a relationship helps us transcend our immediate feelings while connecting us with some higher good.

Awakening the Mind of Peace

When Peace Is the Purpose

Some years ago, in our first conflict resolution workshop in Cyprus involving both Greek Cypriots and Turkish Cypriots, I had the occasion to see a concrete example of the principle of relationship on purpose.

Realizing that these two groups of people had likely not met or spoken with anyone from the other side in more than twenty years, I understood that their first efforts at dialogue could conceivably break apart on contact with sensitive issues and strong emotions from the past. In such situations, I often suggest that people make an effort to "stay through the hard places." We have a natural tendency, when things get tense, to walk away, sometimes in righteous indignation, with some version of, "If that's how you're going to be, I'm leaving!"

"Staying through the hard places" means making a conscious decision to forgo the momentary satisfaction of leaving, choosing instead to remain with the pain to see what might be beyond it. Indeed, the more we want to run away, the more likely it is that we will experience some important learning just on the other side of that resistance.

In the first round of dialogue, people were asked to listen to one another speak about whatever was important to them about the Cyprus situation. They were encouraged not to answer back, but rather seek only to understand how each speaker's words made sense to them. Each, they were assured, would have the opportunity to speak.

Katie, a Greek Cypriot woman whose husband's family had become refugees during the violent events in Cyprus in 1974, started off by telling about the pain of that time. She spoke of how her husband's family was forced to flee the advancing Turkish troops, leaving their ancestral home and lands, and of how many family members have been missing since then.

A Turkish Cypriot man listened carefully. When it was his turn to share, he spoke of the same events of 1974 from his point of view, rejoicing in the presence of Turkish troops as a liberation and protection force, freeing his community from the threat of conquest or destruction by the Greeks.

Later in the workshop, I asked if anyone had had to practice the suggestion of staying through the hard places. Katie raised her hand. She said that she had been profoundly hurt and angry when her dialogue partner spoke positively of events that she had just described as deeply painful. She had wanted to leave the workshop and never come back. I asked why she had stayed. "I realized," she said, "that if I want peace on this island, I can love this man as I love any human being, even if I disagree with him, no matter how painful or hard it might be."

Katie had set her purpose before her eyes, and used it as a guidepost along a difficult journey. I'm sure she, and other peacebuilders like her in Cyprus and elsewhere, have had to come again and again to the remembrance of their aspirations to keep themselves going through the many hard places in rebuilding broken relationships. From that day several years ago, Katie has gone on to become one of the strongest lights in the citizen peacebuilding movement in Cyprus, having personally convened hundreds of people in both communities for dialogue and bridge-building activities, despite numerous threats against her life and her children. Her purpose and her vision allow her to transcend the hardships of the journey. She has a star to steer by.

Awakening the Mind of Peace

Conflict as Spiritual Growth

There is another element of purpose we can pay attention to in shaping the quality of our relationships, particularly when they get difficult, and that is the element of spiritual growth. Since we are always in relationship, relationship is one of our strongest vehicles for learning the lessons through which we evolve as spiritual beings.

Relationships, especially with those close to us, are not always easy. Problems, difficulties, conflicts arise. We get angry; we feel hurt, betrayed, unloved. We resort to one or both of our two favorite strategies: fight or flight. Neither strategy is likely to improve the quality of the relationship over the long term, though a fight might clear the air temporarily, or flight might allow some breathing space for the parties to calm down.

In other words, conflicts in our relationships, whether one-on-one or between groups, are a natural part of human experience. When that conflict is seen as an opportunity for learning and growth—that is, when learning becomes the purpose—then the energy of the relationship can be channeled toward that purpose in a positive way.

All of us have lessons to learn in our spiritual evolution. For someone else, the story of the relationship with the husband of my best friend may have had a very different ending. It may have been more important to their growth that they learn to stay in the conflict and work it out. For me, the lesson was in remembering I could love him while choosing to leave a situation that was not nourishing to anyone. It was also about remembering that conflict is an opportunity for opening my heart.

At first, as our disagreements grew more heated, I would come home and rail against this man in my mind. I would think of all the things I should have said or done. I would analyze his many faults. I would feel all roiled up inside. Only after I asked myself what the opportunity for learning might be in this circumstance did I begin to change. I understood that it was an opportunity to learn to "love my enemy," not as some hypothetical moral principle but as a real transformation.

Gradually, I set myself the practice of imagining a beam of pure love moving from my heart to his. I was completely unable to accomplish this for many weeks, because I was so angry and upset. Love and anger cannot exist in the same place at exactly the same time, I discovered. Only slowly, bit by bit, was I able to see that beam of light, and hold it for a brief moment, before the turmoil would come crashing back. When I was finally able to hold it for several seconds at a time, I realized that I could let the business go. My partnership with this man was not a mistake or a failure. On the contrary, it was a blessing that allowed me to learn valuable lessons about love and anger and the power of friendship.

To say that each of us has our own life lessons does not mean that we are adrift in our relationships without a rudder to steer us toward our highest good. All our faith systems have guidelines for how we are to grow into what my teacher calls "dignified human beings." And some of us have already mastered lessons that, to others of us, may seem impossible.

I have discovered that my spiritual growth usually consists of taking the next step in one of four areas: listening to the "still small voice within"; opening my heart; letting go to trust the universe; or taking responsibility for my thoughts, words, and deeds. That experience with my business partner took me further into all these places than I had been before. I consider that a blessing.

The Power of Partnership

While we each as individuals have our own cutting edge of spiritual growth, so too do we as a human family have lessons to learn. After thirty years of bearing witness to individual, family, group, and intergroup relationships at the local and international levels, I have concluded that the edge of our collective learning has to do with the power relationships we construct with one another.

I have come to believe that the root choice we make in any relationship has to do with power. We can choose to be in a relationship where one party seeks to dominate, control, or otherwise seek power over another, or we can be in a relationship where the parties relate from an equal footing, using their power together to benefit each other and those around them. Riane Eisler, in her magnificent book, *The Chalice and the Blade,* introduced the notion of dominator and partnership cultures, terms that describe these two patterns.

Within each of these models, obviously, there is a continuum. In the dominance relationship, the level of control may be socially acceptable, as between parents and children in some societies; it may be subtle, as in a friendship where each friend wants to be the leader or decision maker; or it may be forceful and violent, as between master and slave, or conqueror and vanquished. Likewise, in the partnership stream, we might find a mutual respect between two parties operating with very different levels of knowledge and responsibility, a simple cooperative effort, or a highly creative, high-performing, and synergistic team.

Ultimately, like Eisler and many others, I believe our evolution as a species depends on our moving from dominance to partnership. We have played out the pattern whereby the strong rule the weak; where humanity is posed against nature; where one gender, culture, religion, or race is considered superior to another and entitled by that superiority to enforce its predominance.

Our history is full of systems of racism, imperialism, sexism, and colonialism based on these assumptions. Our current headlines show increasing extremes of these attitudes among various groups. However, I think we've come to the end of the evolutionary stream built around dominance. Now we are starting to reap the inevitable bitter fruits of such behavior, and to learn hard lessons from the backlash.

Again, the natural world is our first teacher, letting us know that our policies of manipulating the Earth's natural resources for our own short-term benefits indeed have a long-term negative payback. We have discovered—at least to some degree—that we cannot continue indefinitely to poison our soil, mine our minerals, or cut our forests. We can see the end result of such policies; indeed, we are already starting to feel the lack engendered by such short-sighted attempts to win in what we have framed as a battle of "man versus nature."

In our human relations, we are also beginning to realize that dominance cannot work over time. Whether in large political systems, like the totalitarian regimes of the former Soviet Union, or in personal relationships in our families, when one spouse rules the other through threats of violence, no one likes to be repressed or controlled by another. We naturally push against such forces, seeking to overcome the weight of that which oppresses us.

In my training workshops, I often use a simple analogy for the dynamics of such a dominance relationship. I invite people to make two fists, and place one over the other as if you were playing "One potato two potato. . . . " What happens when you push down with the upper fist? Naturally, the lower fist pushes back up, to counter that thrust. When I invite people to describe what this feels like, they indicate that the lower fist wants to get away, or preferably, to "win" and get on top. Further, they say that this relationship is extremely tiring, using all the energy of their hands to keep the other in check. The top fist is concerned with staying on top, while the bottom wants to free itself and take over the top position. This is a set-up for an endless cycle of revolution and power struggle.

I once was consulting with a large company in the southern United States, in a state formerly associated with the Confederacy, on the subject of diversity. Whites and blacks were discussing racial issues in the workplace. At one point, we asked the white men to sit together in the center of the circle to discuss their particular concerns. When they did that, their conversation with each other changed, taking on a cautious tone, as if something were scaring them. With encouragement to speak about what was happening, they eventually acknowledged being uncomfortable surrounded by, and having their backs to, a group of black men, even though the white men far outnumbered and out-ranked the blacks in the room (and in the company).

In that moment I felt the ghosts of slavery in the room with us. Slave owners always had to be looking over their shoulders, waiting for the insurrection that must surely be brewing among their slaves. They knew that even though they controlled the blacks completely through the force of whips, chains, and law, they were never safe from the inevitable backlash. They understood, in other words, that dominance is inherently unstable. The oppressed will always, like the bottom fist, seek to gain its freedom, either by getting out from under or, more likely, by turning the tables and rising to the top.

So dominance, ultimately, doesn't work. Whether in our family lives or on the international scene, dominance leads to recurring cycles of violence, revenge, revolution, and the breakdown of order. This should not surprise us, since dominance, being based in separation and superiority rather than aligned with the truth of our sacred oneness, has within it the seed of its own destruction. If there is only one whole, any single part of that unity, in seeking to impose its will on another, is actually harming itself and the whole.

Michael Burkart, from Amherst, Massachusetts, describes the harmful effects of being, as a white male, part of the dominant culture.

Men lose their humanity because it has become so narrowly defined by all the things we are not allowed to do: feel our emotions, explore the feminine aspect of our nature, access our intuition. In being cut off from these aspects of ourselves, we are cut off from the whole, and then can only respond in limited ways—as with war, sports, competition, and hard-driving linear approaches.

I have learned about the price I pay being a white man from working with strong women—white women and women of color. They can do what I can do, but I can't do what they can do. I learned from watching them that making connection with people is more important than being smart or right.

Awakening the Mind of Peace

As men we are taught that our primary relationships occur with other men as we engage in doing things: sports, war, playing cards, business. Women are relegated to sexual objects that we need for sex, but not true intimacy. What other men think is always more important. Hence, we don't exercise social or moral courage. We will run into a burning building to save people, but we won't risk being ostracized from the group of men.

I have learned to understand this and accept the feminine side of my being through experiences in nature. In nature, everything is connected. What's alive is pliable. What's dead is stiff. To belong with the oppressor, to deaden our feelings, is to be stiff.

Dominance therefore, is not right relationship, and the longer we, as individuals or as a species, remain attached to this mode in our relationships with each other and with the Earth, we are guaranteeing that we, or our children and grandchildren, will suffer the negative consequences of those actions.

We already are suffering those consequences on a large scale. Global warming, the rise of failed states and transnational terrorism, the ethnic, racial, and religious wars around the world, the increase in domestic and sexual violence that we witness day by day—these are indications of forms losing their integrity. Systems that were built on domination are breaking down in these times, giving humanity a rare opportunity to build new systems based on true assumptions, the premise of partnership.

Partnership is a relationship whose motto could be, "We're all in this together!" It arises from an awareness of our interrelatedness. In a partnership, power is shared. Rather than seeking power over another, we seek power *with* each other, understanding that one and one result in something greater than two.

To go back to the hand analogy, a partnership is like the two hands open to each other, fingers, wrists, even arms interacting in various creative and cooperative ways, to make something that will benefit the larger whole. Each brings its resources to the interaction; each gains something useful. Together the two may generate something unexpected, something that grows from the unique interplay of the moment.

In partnerships, energy is utilized creatively. Not having to be spent in an unending game of pressure and counterpressure, energy is available to shape the relationship according to its highest purpose. For instance, when I stopped fighting with my business partner, and stopped tearing myself apart at home by rehashing every detail of our struggle, I was able to remember what was truly important to me, and reshape the relationship along those lines.

A partnership is not about sameness but about sharing. We do not, any of us, have the same life paths, the same wisdom, or personal resources. We have multiple differences. But whoever we are and whatever we bring, we can bring fully to the relationship, rather than hoarding or hiding our resources from one other, or using them to hurt each other. We can honor each other as equals, and treat all parties with respect, within the bounty of our diversity.

Even as old forms of dominance are falling away, new forms in the partnership mode are appearing. We see citizen coalitions in communities all across America, working together to solve local problems. We see diversity programs in schools and companies, as people seek to establish dialogue across gender, racial, and ethnic lines. Our children are learning conflict resolution and mediation in school, so they can solve their own problems amicably, instead of through fighting.

On a global scale, we see efforts at building large systems of cooperation, like the European Union, where many smaller units working together and pooling their resources can magnify the benefits to vastly larger numbers of people. Domestically, this has its mirror image in the many co-ops—for food or banking, housing or health care—that are growing up in our cities and towns.

Relationships based on dominance create conflict. They ultimately lead to violence, coercion, and war. Relationships based on partnership create peace. They ultimately lead to cooperation, sharing, and building. When framed in this way, it sounds like a simple choice. If it were easy to abandon one for the other, we would simply do it.

Unfortunately, so many institutions of modern life are mired deeply in the assumptions of the separative mind that leads to dominance that the change is not an easy one. We are in the midst of the transformation, and are not yet totally free of the old ways of thinking. We still live, most of us, in what I call conflict-habituated systems, deeply embedded habits of not being in right relationship to each other, that act like powerful default settings, pulling us back to the familiar even when we wish to change.

When I was growing up, my greatest "enemy" was my older brother. Whatever it was about my being that touched off a rage within him, he found my presence highly threatening from the day I came home from the hospital as an infant. For many years, he acted out his fear and anger through various forms of physical and emotional violence.

As we both grew to adulthood, he could more clearly see the damage this was doing, to me and to himself, and he tried to change. I have a vivid memory of us as young adults, sitting at the kitchen table of our family home, discussing this situation frankly. In a very poignant moment, he apologized for the harm he had caused. I forgave him. We were both deeply touched. We hugged. Then, in that instant, the old cloud passed over his face, and he was driven to say, "I'm sorry for how I used to beat you up—but you know, I could still do it if I wanted to!" He just couldn't let go fully. At least, not then.

Hard as it may seem to change these patterns, the switch to relations based on partnership is, I believe, our current evolutionary challenge. Our doorway to individual and collective spiritual growth, this opportunity to realign ourselves with a greater good must prevail if we are to survive on this planet.

Peace Is a Family Affair

What happens on a planetary level is a reflection of what happens in our hearts and homes, for our individual lives are the microcosm within which these larger forces of evolution are playing themselves out on a daily basis. One of the truths I have discovered through the decades of peacebuilding work is that we tend to fight the most with those to whom we have the deepest connection. Most of our major conflicts are family feuds, whether at the personal or at the group level.

The Israelis are not in conflict with the Indonesians, although many in Indonesia are Muslim. The Israelis are in conflict with their direct neighbors, the Palestinians and other Arab countries, who are also their cousins, sharing as they do a common ancestor, Abraham, and a common land. The Tutsis are not in conflict with the Somalis, though they share many regional concerns. They are in conflict with the Hutus, with whom they have seesawed back and forth for many decades over issues of power and property.

This is not just about the closeness of geography, but about the intimacy of relationships that will not go away. We care the most about those with whom we share some basic element of our lives and always will: the same land, a parent or ancestor, a culture, a history of victimhood. That doesn't mean we don't have major differences with our conflict partners. On the contrary, we have big differences, but it is those overlapping places of intimacy, plus the continuity of the relationship, that make the fight so meaningful.

We first learn about relationship in our immediate families of origin. Growing up in our particular nuclear and extended families teaches us what it means to be related, and how relatives are with each other. This is where we first learn about boundaries, and about who is one of "us" and who is outside our circle, one of "them." Depending on the circumstances in which this message comes to us, we will shape how we see those who are different from us.

Some families operate with a strong centripetal force, bringing their members into a tightly knit, core family unit. Others operate with a centrifugal force, sending their members out into the larger world with more loosely knit ties to one another. Most families probably find themselves somewhere in the center of this continuum. The attitude with which these constellations are communicated will determine how we view our own identity vis-à-vis others. If our family is very close, and deeply bonded through love, we may feel the group strength to reach out to include others in that love. If the closeness is based more on a desire to protect the group from external threats, we may feel that strangers are not to be trusted.

Whatever conclusions we draw, we all do have some (often uncon-scious) way of discerning "us" from "them," "me" from "the other." If this relationship is seen as benign or friendly, the tension between who is inside and who is outside can be creative. If the relationship is seen as unfriendly or threatening, we have the potential for isolation, alienation, or adversarial conflict.

Families are also where we get our basic human needs met—or not. Adapting the famous work of Abraham Maslow, these needs can be described as security, identity, community, and vitality. That is, we all need to know that we walk safely in the world, without fear of vio-lence against our person or our psyche, and that we can be fed, shel-tered, and clothed appropriately. On top of that, we need to feel self-esteem and worthiness, and to know that we are a part of a social unit larger than ourselves that recognizes, includes, and honors our unique identity. Beyond that, we need to have meaning in our lives, and to grow spiritually as well as mentally, emotionally, and physically, in order to realize our highest potential.

We are dependent on our loved ones for getting these needs met, and therefore are more vulnerable with them than with strangers. Our family's opinion of us, their caring for us, their behavior toward us, are central to our well-being. So if our needs are not satisfactorily met, or worse, if they are purposefully violated by those we cherish, a hole is torn in the fabric of our being. A casual derogatory remark from a classmate may hurt our feelings; that same derogatory remark from a parent or sibling may be devastating.

The same is true of group-level families. The group or groups I identify with (such as women, people with the same religion, others in my professional field) provide my sense of place in the world, and give

Awakening the Mind of Peace

meaning to my life experience. Our intergroup life—interactions and attitudes between ethnic, racial, gender, religious, geographic, or other such identity groups—displays those same family dynamics, only on a larger scale.

So thinking of right relationship means thinking about how we are in our families—the original families of our childhood, the families we create as adults, the families we participate in through group identity. These are the places where we learn our patterns, the places we repeat our patterns, and the places we can correct our patterns of relationship. If peace begins with me, then I must begin with my family.

Of Victims and Villains

Two typical patterns that arise from our family life, whether from our nuclear families or from our larger identity groups, concern the creation of victims and villains. We are the victim; the "other" is the villain.

These are archetypal figures in the human melodrama that is at the core of our cultural identity. Whenever we tell or hear stories that have meaning for us—through our history, novels, drama, television shows, sermons, songs, news accounts—we are likely to portray some version of victim or enemy, or both.

Stereotypical victims occupy a certain moral high ground, being faultless recipients of another's hurtful behavior. They are innocent. They are likable. They draw on our heartstrings. They need help from stronger figures, from some type of rescuer. For this help, they are grateful.

Stereotypical villains, on the other hand, are unlikable. They are bad, mean, scary people or groups who will deliberately cause pain and suffering. They are evil. Enemies are to be vanquished or overcome. We rejoice in their defeat. Some enemies are so good at being vile, we want to keep them around for further bashing, like Superman's Lex Luthor.

Victims and villains need each other. It is their relationship, the constant interplay of exploiter and exploited, that calls for the hero, the one who comes to the rescue. The stereotypical rescuer is resolute and fearless, wise and powerful—a reliable champion for the underdog. We cheer when the hero (or heroine) enters the stage.

Just as the victim is the projection of all our fears and helplessness, and the villain is the vessel into which we pour all our baseness, so the hero is the projection of all our virtue, our goodness, our power over the dark forces. In a satisfying story, the hero always wins.

The phenomenon of projection is important here, because we use it to separate ourselves from our inherent wholeness. The parts of ourselves that we would rather not acknowledge, we project onto others, keeping for ourselves only those parts that are comfortable. In this way we polarize ourselves inside, but see this polarization only as something outside us. Unable to reinternalize those aspects of ourselves we have projected onto others, we condemn ourselves to repeating the same melodramatic cycles endlessly.

We are all familiar with the typical melodrama that epitomizes these patterns, where the villain ties the maiden to the railroad tracks because she will not give up her "virtue" to him. Naturally, the hero arrives just in time, frees the maiden, and defeats the villain in a show of victory of good over evil. We have heard this plot line so many times, in so many variations, that we can easily and unconsciously fall into the ritual set of relationships of victim, villain, and hero that, in the psychological world, is called the drama triangle.

Awakening the Mind of Peace

This set of relationships is considered a triangle because the roles often rotate. That is, when the heroine comes to the rescue by challenging the persecutor, the villain then becomes the victim, and the heroine is seen as the new persecutor. One who is the victim may easily become the enemy by striking back in anger. The plot stays the same; the actors simply shift roles.

Rarely in our lives do we play out these roles so starkly. Nonetheless, we all have different levels of familiarity with one or another of these roles. As individuals and as groups, we tend toward seeing ourselves a certain way on the world stage, or in the family saga. Raised in a Jewish family and regularly assaulted by my brother, for example, I am myself familiar, both personally and ethnically, with the victim role.

In the story we tell ourselves in the United States, we are the superpower, the hero poised to save the rest of the world. In this story line, we have cast various religious extremists (particularly Islamic groups) as one set of evil villains, while in the story they tell themselves, we of course are the satanic forces and they are the bearers of Light.

These roles are more than hollow labels, however. They carry some germ of the truth of our experience, or else we wouldn't continue to energize them so widely. It is true that many of us, as individuals or groups, have indeed experienced uninvited abuse from others. We truly are victims of violence. It is also true that there are perpetrators of aggression—people who do plant bombs, invade one another's territory, molest trusting young children. And surely there are people who have, at great risk to themselves, saved others from such harm; there are actual heroes in the world.

I do not mean to demean these roles, only to point out how easily they become containers in which we find ourselves trapped within a narrow range of human experience. If we become used to thinking about ourselves in these ways, we respond unthinkingly and automatically, and miss the opportunity to explore a far vaster set of potential relationships. If we lock ourselves in to the melodrama model, we are not free to explore the possibilities for transformation and right relationship. In addition, we are fueling an adversarial mindset that energizes and sustains the polarization of relationship.

In my work around the world, in places of harsh suffering and recurring cycles of conflict, as well as with families and communities struggling to find that better way, I have found three interesting phenomena relating to these roles. First, there is a subtle way in which some (though obviously not all) people who have been profoundly harmed cross the line from being someone who is in pain to being someone who defines their identity by their pain. In this scenario, our sense of victimhood becomes a cherished badge of honor. Our suffering makes us noble, or worthy of attention, or deserving of aid. It's almost as if our victim status gives us a certain importance, without which we may not be able to survive our tragedies.

A second aspect of this is what I call "the yardstick of suffering." Here we compare our suffering to others, and it is very important to us that our pain measures higher on the measuring stick. Somehow, our victim role is threatened or diminished if someone else can claim the same or greater degree of hurt.

Finally, I am aware of mutual projection, by which, in a conflict, both sides see themselves as the victim and the other as the villain. They might as well be mirrors to each other, not only repeating what was done to them, but acknowledging their own actions only in the other, not in themselves. Anyone outside this situation can see the parallelism of it, and the inevitable cycle of stalemate or escalation that it produces. Anyone inside such a situation sees only that the other side is the enemy.

These patterns could be seen as humorous examples of the human condition, if they weren't so dangerous. They are dangerous because, when we are attached to seeing ourselves as victims and the other as our enemy, we are shackled into ways of relating that perpetuate hatred, fear, and violence. People in these states are easily manipulated by irresponsible leaders, who stir up passions for revenge, riot, or mayhem against the other.

When we perceive others as the enemy, we demonize them. We call them names, ascribe negative characteristics to them, make them less than human. "They don't value life the way we do," we say, or "They don't even feel pain like regular people." In this way we can justify to ourselves the right, indeed the need, to destroy them or strike against them. If we saw them as like "us," or recognized our human communion, compassion would replace hatred, and then we would be surrendering our identity as victims and theirs as enemy.

Ultimately, these patterns are dangerous because of the long-term harm they engender. When we pass on this way of relating as victims and villains to our children and grandchildren, the fear and hatred, the myths and the stereotypes, become intergenerational, and therefore much harder to change. Even worse, the adversarial approach to relationships is reinforced, and the illusion of separation is strengthened.

We may be most familiar with this pattern in news reports from the Middle East, perhaps, or from Rwanda or the Balkans. It is far easier to identify such behavior in faraway places rather than in ourselves. Yet these same patterns are being played out regularly, perhaps to a lesser degree, in our home lives, in our cities, and in our political system.

In Buddhism, it is said that human suffering, which is universal, arises from three afflicting emotions: ignorance, attachment, and repulsion. In this view, ignorance refers to seeing only the part and not the whole; thinking of ourselves as individual beings separate from the rest of an interdependent web of creation; not recognizing our innate divine wisdom. Attachment refers to our desire to hold on to things that we like—beliefs, opinions, people, possessions, situations. Repulsion is the opposite, a pushing away of those things or people or situations we don't like. Attachment is an expression of greed; repulsion leads to aggression, hatred, and anger. Both afflict us with constant suffering because we fail to see the basic nature of impermanence, and believe that we can force or control life to give us what we want.

In relationships, we are caught in ignorance when we deny our innate oneness or wholeness. We are caught in attachment and repulsion when we are engaged in this seesaw of victims and villains. Our work, in seeking the Spirit of Peace, is to break free of the polarization of "us" and "them," realizing that I and the other are one. Only by embracing the enemy we have created in our mind can we move proactively rather than reactively to create right relationship in our lives. This is just as true in a fight we may be having with our spouse or with a colleague at work as it is between the Serbs and the ethnic Albanians.

Witness at Dachau

Sometimes, embracing the enemy is particularly hard. In 1991, I visited Dachau. My family on both sides came to America from the Jewish

Awakening the Mind of Peace

shtetls of Eastern Europe at the turn of the century, so none of my immediate family was lost in the Holocaust. Still, there is tribal memory. After my trip, I put some of my thoughts in writing, and published these reflections originally in *Pathways,* a quarterly journal in the Washington, D.C., area.

Dachau is stark, bare and gray, even on a sunny day. Within the walls and watchtowers, not much is left of the physical buildings of the camp: only the administration building, two barracks, the crematorium. Even the memorials and shrines built by religious groups are cold and unforgiving. Only a convent next door, opening its chapel for prayer, offers a place of human softness, of spiritual solace.

The physical space is dominated by an empty gravel plaza in front of the barracks. Here was the place of roll call, of control and punishment. Though the buildings are empty, the plaza is not. It is filled with ghosts.

I wanted to run off into the woods, to find a quiet, green, and peaceful spot where I could embrace the pain, release the flood of tears. But the inmates of Dachau had no place to run, no place to hide, so I too stayed in the open square. I stood at attention with the ghosts of this place. When they call the numbers of the roll, I will be here. When they choose whom to shoot; whom to flog; whom to hang from the trees by the wrists, with arms twisted behind their backs; whom to work to death—I will be here, in full sight, present, at attention.

I will be a conscious witness to one of the most concentrated, coordinated acts of cruelty that we know of, and I will not flinch or shrink away, though I would prefer to run as far away as possible. I will stare into the face of evil, eye to eye, and though my heart longs to take up the cry "Never again!" I refuse myself that luxury, because I do not believe humanity is yet ready to take that stand.

Genocide—the planned slaughter, torture, imprisonment, cultural destruction, starvation, or degradation of masses of people whose color, religion, tribe, ethnic or national identity, or political beliefs are "wrong"—continues around the world. We take most note of it when it affects our own people, our close neighbors, our strategic interests, or when its scale is large enough to get our attention. For other occasions, like in Cambodia, Tibet, or with the indigenous peoples all over the world, we find excuses, we ignore, we shake our heads and murmur sad phrases. So how can we say "Never again," when it seems to be ever and ever again and again our way, as human beings, to kill and oppress others when it suits our perceived interests?

One of the scariest, most appalling aspects of the Holocaust was how systematically it was enacted. In the museum at Dachau is a huge wall chart, showing all the prison and extermination camps throughout Europe, and all their auxiliary and feeder camps. I never knew about those auxiliary camps before—there appear to be hundreds of them. I learned too that even the smallest details of camp life were centrally planned and promulgated. The Nazis were rigorous about the business of mass murder. But the tragedies in Liberia, Sudan, Guatemala, El Salvador, Northern Ireland, Sri Lanka, and elsewhere are no less horrendous for being less visible, for touching fewer lives, for passing under the rubric of political conflict rather than genocide.

Humanity's present cry may well be not "Never again" but "Not in my backyard," for the killing and inhumane behavior continues in these days in the East Timors and Rwandas of the world, and we set up hardly a whimper. But the ghosts of Dachau are howling.

Awakening the Mind of Peace

Before I actually arrived there, I thought it was a shame to continue to energize such a memorial. Better, perhaps, to plant trees and flowers to remember the dead, thereby transforming the energy. Part of me still believes that. Now that I've been to Dachau, however, and experienced the power of the ghosts, I understand the need for education. If every citizen of the world could pass through a place such as this and hear that howling for themselves, then perhaps we could raze all the death camps and plant flower gardens.

As I stood in the plaza, I found myself praying for the prisoners of Dachau: May they be released from their suffering. I prayed for their families as well, and especially for those who survived, for now I begin to understand the "survivor's guilt" syndrome—I felt it a bit myself just standing there.

Then I was surprised to find myself praying also for the guards and commandants, the planners and perpetrators of this outrage. What distortion, what ignorance, what mindlessness, what poverty of spirit must have been their lot, that they could visit these horrors on other human beings? If the ghosts of the inmates were howling, the souls of the staff must be shrieking with the hell they had called down upon themselves. I prayed that they all, we all, may be released from the gray light of this torture, and find the road of peace again.

The only place I knew to look for that peace, as I stood in the roll call plaza, was in my own heart. I wept, I breathed, I affirmed that I and all people are inherently divine human beings. I embraced all the lost souls of this place, for it is only in our unity that I can find a small spark of hope. I called on the Light for a blessing. I think—I hope—it helped.

I Am the Other

To find the "other" beyond the villain label, we may need to first soften our own victim stance. When I first went to Israel and the Occupied Territories in 1988, I spent considerable time in the West Bank and Gaza, trying to understand the situation from the Palestinian point of view. Since I was born into a Jewish American family in 1944, I essentially grew up alongside the State of Israel, cheering for its victories, grieving for its losses. Entering the Palestinian world was, for me, entering enemy territory, yet I knew I had to encompass all views if I were to become a true peacebuilder.

I remember an early moment in that journey. I was sitting in the home of a Palestinian family during the Intifada, experiencing with them the hardship of living under Israeli military occupation. As gracious and generous as the family was, I still felt uneasy. Then, my host expressed a most astounding thought. "We don't hate the Jews," he said. "We don't want to push them into the sea. We only want to live side by side with them, in peace and respect."

My internal voice immediately shouted, "Oh yeah? What a lie! I don't believe that for a minute!" Having heard the opposite about Palestinians for forty years, there was no way I could credit any truth to that statement.

Over the next few days, however, as I met more people from that family and community, I heard variations of that statement many times. Each time I could feel the words bounce off the hard knot in my mind and heart that had been trained to believe that all Arabs hated all Jews and, like many nations throughout history, wished for our extinction.

Gradually, I began to ask myself, "Could this possibly be true? Could some, maybe many, perhaps even most Palestinians, want to live peacefully, as neighbors, with Israelis?"

Slowly, slowly, over time, I allowed the witness of my eyes and of my direct experience of these wonderful people to soften that hard knot. As it dissolved, so did the image of the enemy I had carried all my life. In its stead grew a clearer, more realistic picture of fellow human beings, just like "us"; living with fear and pain, just like "us"; wanting peace, just like "us"; caught in a violent cycle of action and reaction, just like "us."

So too did the image of the victim begin to shift. When I saw not just what "they" had done to "us," but at the same time what "we" were doing to "them," I began to understand the real meaning of the phrase "common ground." Truly, these were people I could walk with, in a shared journey toward peace.

That was the beginning of what has been, and still is, a very rich journey indeed. For over a decade, I have been privileged to be a bridge between Israelis and Palestinians. I work in both societies, with deep friendships on either side. From refugee camps in Gaza, the religious settlements near Jerusalem, a kibbutz in the Israeli countryside, Palestinian villages in the West Bank, Palestinian-Israeli towns in the Galilee, the streets and markets of both East and West Jerusalem, the religious shrines and holy sites of Christianity, Judaism, and Islam— from all these places I have learned to understand the frustrations, the dreams, the fear, and the pain of both communities.

I can convene meetings between them, because I recognize that there are no stereotypical victims or villains or rescuers here—only people who have been at both the giving and receiving end of pain, struggling to find a better way. While I do not agree with or approve of those on either side who are seeking s solution through violence or domination, I can function as a peacebuilder knowing that I and the "other" are one in this holy land.

This knowledge grew through many experiences of my own—both bitter and beautiful. I have been at the wrong end of a soldier's gun; caught in the melee and tear gas of a police action; had my car stoned with me inside; and watched helplessly as my hosts and friends have been arrested. I have witnessed the grief of families on both sides when they lost sons to the conflict. I have faced my own reactive rage and judgment against those whose approaches to the peace process I find distasteful.

At the same time, I have celebrated the national days and religious festivals of both groups. I've observed Christmas Mass in Bethlehem, Passover in Jerusalem, and Ramadan in Nazareth. I have received the gracious hospitality of households wealthy and poor, but always rich in kindness. I have seen miracles of hope and courage, as brave people committed to peace on both sides have shown me their projects, spilled their dreams into my hands. I have heard the wind sing across the hilltops, smelled the perfume of orange blossoms in the night air, and found solace in a grove of ancient olive trees.

In short, I have lived, if ever so briefly and superficially, within the skin of Israelis and Palestinians across the whole range of the religious and political spectrum, and in all corners of the land. The collapse of my victim/villain mindset, however, was completed only on the night I was warmly and generously adopted into a Palestinian family. Then, and only then, did I know without a doubt that I was both a daughter of Israel and a sister of Palestine. Then, and only then, did I truly understand that there is no "other"; there is only the one that we are. Which is simply divine.

A Mountain of Lies

What gets in the way of truly realizing this truth, that I and the other are one? I was greatly struck by an image that arose during a workshop in a country with a long history of ethnic conflict. This workshop was supposed to be the first meeting of people from the two sides, for training in conflict resolution. However, the day before the event, there was a political crisis, and conditions did not allow for a meeting of the two groups. Instead, we chose to meet first with one group, then the other, bringing their messages to one another in a kind of citizen shuttle diplomacy.

In one of the groups, someone spoke of a mountain of lies that stood between the two communities. In exploring this image, we heard that the mountain was built of all the myths and stereotypes, all the unhealed wounds of history, all the extreme chauvinistic rhetoric, all the memories of injustice and atrocities, all the accumulated fear, hatred, and anguish of the people.

Most mountains are made by the forces of nature. This one was created by violent forces of human nature. The stones in this mountain were raised by the interplay of a sensationalized press, distorted schoolbooks, nationalistic exhortations, entrenched interests, the games and intrigues of international power politics, and the clashing needs and desires of various peoples and countries over many decades.

This mountain, which blocks the view and the passage between us, does not exist only in the country I was then working in. In families and communities everywhere we have some version of this heavy pile of refuse. These mountains are no more than a pile of rubble, held together by the sticks and stones of dusty memory and countless tales of victimhood and villainy.

In realizing this, we realize our task as peacebuilders. We can attempt to disassemble the mountain, stone by stone, or climb to its peak and look across to the other side. We can seek a road around it, or carve a path through its center, or perhaps discover a natural pass through hidden valleys. Whatever choice we make, the work is to get beyond the mountain of lies, to see each other as we really are, in the present, and see what we can do together for a better future.

To See Each Other As We Really Are

We cannot make right relationship if we cannot know each other truly. This means we need to make authentic human contact, heart to heart and mind to mind, and discover how we each make sense to ourselves. Only then can we cross through the mountain of lies to find a better way to build peace.

One day I was wandering among the orchards on one of Cyprus' beautiful hillsides, and was admiring the simple, utilitarian stone waterworks built to capture and distribute water that came from several small springs. Across the face of the hill ran an open stone pipe from which, at intervals, other open troughs were laid downhill, to run streams of water to the fields below. Each of these troughs was controlled by a simple gate, a piece of metal in a slot which, when raised, would allow the water to flow through from the horizontal pipe.

Awakening the Mind of Peace

I saw one such water gate that was stuck partly open, its bottom space filled with rubble of stones, twigs, and mud. I realized that the removal of a few sticks, a vigorous shaking to release dried mud, and the whole ball of debris would fall easily apart, allowing the waters to course through the pipes to irrigate the parched fields.

I realized this was a lesson for me about peacemaking—that the debris which obscures the passage of the waters of peace can be shaken loose, if we can find just the right twigs to remove. Though I know we could name many such twigs that hold the debris together in our relationship patterns, I have identified four which I think are significant in either preventing or allowing us to truly meet and understand one another: our pain, our choices, our truths, and our wholeness. Shaking ourselves free in these areas, we release ourselves as hostages to the limited mind of "us" and "them," and begin to see each other clearly, without distortion, in all our human frailty and divine perfection. When we can truly meet one another in this way, the rivers of right relationship can flow freely to the vast and endless ocean of peace.

Through the Lens of Our Pain

We are all the center of our own universes, whether we think individualisticly or communally. What happens to me or to my group holds the central place in my thinking. Anyone else's experience is naturally a secondary matter of concern for me.

This is especially true in the matter of suffering. For each of us, our unique suffering is paramount. How we actually deal with our pain, and transmute our suffering, is something we will talk about in the next chapter. Here, however, as we discuss right relationship, it is important to consider how we hold that pain in the context of our relationships.

We want others to acknowledge our pain and to fix their attention on it, just as we are doing. We don't want to—in many cases are not able to—listen to another's story. Our own fills our inner space, and any space between us.

In the dialogues I do with groups in conflict, I often ask people to think of coming together with one another while holding an imaginary glass of water that contains the truth of one's own experience. If I approach another person with a full glass, I have no room to receive their truth. If I come with an empty glass, I have nothing to share. If I come with a partially filled glass, there is room for mixing and meeting one another.

When we are in pain, however, and especially when that pain has been a result of the relationship we're seeking to heal, the hurt fills the glass. It is extremely difficult to put the glass to the side long enough to hear someone else's story. Anger being the other side of pain, we may even prefer to hurl the hurt at the other, drenching them in our rage. Sometimes, however, we can have an authentic meeting by being fully present with all the pain, and facing into it directly. By going into the pain rather than finding a way to avoid it, we may find a way to move to a new place with our experience.

I saw this once in a dialogue between two groups of people whose communities had been mired in a long and bloody conflict. A woman from one side shared a painful story about being nearby when a terrorist bomb went off in a busy city street, killing and maiming many. She rushed to the scene, and witnessed the bloody horror of it all. She described it in detail, and in tears.

Awakening the Mind of Peace

Her dialogue partner, a man from the other community, was silent for some time. Then he started telling about his mother. He told how she had lost her husband and sons to war, to prison, and to violence with soldiers from the other side. He told how she struggled to find enough food to feed her children. Through the voice of his own anguish, he described his mother's pain.

A witness to this dialogue was very upset. "He wasn't supposed to tell his own story," she lamented. "He was supposed to listen to hers." The man responded, "In my culture, we don't speak about our mothers to strangers. Never. But when I heard the pain of this woman, I wanted to let her know I really understood. I wanted to give her back my own deepest pain, as the most special gift I could think of in return for the gift that she gave me."

Being present to our own pain is hard enough. Being present to the pain of the "other" is an even greater challenge. Without that willingness to let the heart be touched by one another, however, we cannot hope to ever reach within the mountain of lies to free the Spirit of Peace.

Through the Lens of Our Choices

A second twig to pull from the debris has to do with the choices we make in our internal dialogues. In every situation, we can choose how to think about the circumstances or the people involved. We often forget we have these choices, being caught in the habitual patterns of the interaction. However, we do have the ability to shift our thinking. This is called reframing.

Reframing is very much like framing a picture. I once wandered in a beautiful garden and found, at various vantage points along the path, picture frames attached to a stand. Some were at knee level, some were waist- or chest-high. The frames were attached with a swivel, allowing them to be moved in various directions. The frames were empty, giving me the opportunity to frame whatever picture I wanted at each site. Tilting the frame one way, I saw a picture of the rose bed. Tilting it slightly differently, I saw the clouds set against a brilliant sky. In another direction, I could frame the roses and the sky, and the hollyhocks too.

Nothing stops us from this reframing process in our relationships except forgetting it is possible, or not being willing to try. Though the pressures and temptations to see things as we have always seen them may be strong, the gift of taking another view can be miraculous. Jo Imlay shares such a story from her experiences in New Zealand.

My husband and I emigrated from the United States to New Zealand four years ago and bought our dream property, fifty acres of coastal forest in a rugged, remote area three hours' drive from the nearest town. The seller assured us we would have access over a farm couple's road, the only route into our property. We were horrified after we moved in when the farmers told us they would not give us permission to use the road.

Our only alternative was to travel by boat, but the logistics and expense of this were mind-boggling. Our very survival seemed at stake, yet we could not shake the farmers' resolve to bar use of their road. Their one compromise was to give us a grace period of three months to make new arrangements.

In vain we tried everything we could think of to continue having road access, including having our property surveyed and getting area maps to see if we could put in a new road that would avoid the farmers' property. But mostly we prayed. From the start, we were determined not to sink into resentment or anger, but rather to shift our entire focus to beaming love and forgiveness to the farmers. This wasn't always easy, but every day we tried to look at the situation through their eyes to understand their point of view.

Previously we would have concentrated on the injustice being done to us, and argued to get our way without much considering the reasons for the farmers' actions. We would have viewed them as our opponents, possibly even as our enemies. But this time we felt strongly led to trust in the power of love and to turn the matter over to God to work out the best solution for both parties.

As the three months neared their end, the couple reluctantly agreed to meet with us once again to discuss our continued desire to have road access. We decided to speak honestly, "from the heart," and to listen carefully and respectfully to whatever they had to say, without arguing or countering their point of view. After nearly an hour of talk, the farmers again said No.

We were devastated, but although we privately vented some anger and hurt to each other, we still tried to beam love and goodwill to our neighbors, and to get on as best we could with arranging boat travel.

Eight days later, the phone rang. It was the farmer, saying that he and his wife had decided it was an untenable situation for us and that we could use the road once a month! I don't think I've ever felt more relieved or happier or more convinced of the tremendous power of love.

In the four years since, we've found out that eight other families also asked for road access, and only we were granted it. We've repeatedly expressed our gratitude to the farm couple in small ways—by hiring their son to work for us during summers, by giving them small gifts at Christmas, and above all by keeping true to our agreement, even though it is sometimes very difficult going off our land but once a month.

Although we're very different families, a growing friendship and mutual respect have developed. Recently they granted us much more liberal road access, and they've come to our aid during a bad flood. We're now thinking of asking them if they'd like to join us in our main mission here, which is to put our land into a permanent public trust so that it will never be developed. There's a corner of their land that would complete a link to a nearby government nature preserve. Knowing the power of love and the goodness of heart of these farmers we once were tempted to consider as enemies, we think they might say Yes to this, too!

Through the Lens of Our Truths

We construct our lives through the stories we tell ourselves. We construct our stories by filtering information, including some pieces, discarding or ignoring others. We select our information based on how we position our frames, and we position our frames based on what we see as truth.

If I frame my life as one long round of victimization, then any experience or information that doesn't fit with that view will not be incorporated into my stories of reality, and any information that is ambiguous will probably be twisted to fit into that framework, even if the fit is not exact. On the other hand, if I frame my life, as I did during my healing process, as full of joy and peace, then I will reinforce that design in selecting the data that I interpret to make meaning in my affairs. This is a natural and usually unconscious process.

We get into trouble in our relationships when we block out whole sections of information about ourselves or about the "other" because it doesn't conform to our preconceived frame. Thus, I was originally unable to believe that any Palestinians could possibly want to live peacefully, side by side, with Israelis. When this happens, we are unable to truly meet each other, because we meet the reflection of our thinking instead.

Once I was sitting with a family from the dominant culture in a country where a minority group was living under hostile military occupation. There was a long history of bloodshed and violence between the two groups, with the minority group seeking its independence and the majority group adamantly refusing. We were watching a television show of interviews with people on both sides, speaking about what might be necessary for a viable peace process.

When someone from the minority group was speaking about how soldiers had entered his home and terrorized, beaten, and humiliated his entire family, including old women and children, the woman I was sitting with leapt out of her chair, pointed her finger at the screen, and angrily declared that this story was a lie! Their young men, the soldiers, would never treat anyone in that way.

Of course, this woman had never been to the section of the country in which this minority was living under these conditions. She had no firsthand knowledge of the situation there, certainly no way of knowing that this kind of treatment was the everyday reality for many in that community. This statement, therefore, must obviously be false, a blatant attempt at propaganda to win world sympathy. The information was screened according to the parameters that existed in this woman's conditioned experience.

She had sons who had been, or would be, soldiers; many of her friends' sons also had been in the army. These were good boys. Her government's policy would never involve gratuitous violence in this way. If anything like what was being alleged was even remotely true, the family that was beaten must have done something awful to deserve it. Her frame simply did not allow the truth of this other family's experience to filter through to her awareness.

Whether in a fight between husband and wife, two groups, or two countries, whenever two parties are in conflict, inevitably they each have the truth of their own experience on the subject under dispute. Because we are the center of our own universe, we naturally assume that our truth is True with a capital T, and another's is a lie, or distortion; it is False. Since our conflict partner is likely having the same thought about us, there are, in fact, multiple truths existing simultaneously. The challenge, then, is to discover the full range of those truths held by each party, and then to see how, together, those strands can be rewoven into a new story that honors the needs of all.

Having our truth acknowledged is very important, and acknowledging the truth of our conflict partner is extremely difficult. To do this, we need to remember that we don't need to surrender our view when we seek to understand the other. We don't have to surrender our pain to hear of another's. But we do need to be open to new information, and to the adjustments that new data might bring to our view. If we erect walls that keep out or fend off the truth of another's experience, the Spirit of Peace has no room to move. Our boundaries need to be, like the membranes of our cells, semi-permeable, so information and energy can flow in both directions.

In my own journey as a peacebuilder, I once had a reframing experience that changed me profoundly. I had incurred a large personal debt while making a film that explored possibilities for peace in a particularly difficult place of ethnic strife. The project was aborted for lack of money before the film was completed. So I had a big debt, and no film to show for it.

Many years later, a friend, Patricia Remele, offered me financial counseling as I joined with my colleague, Ambassador John McDonald, to open the Institute for Multi-Track Diplomacy in Washington, D.C., to do peacebuilding work around the world. She asked me first to express any beliefs I might already be carrying about money for peace efforts. I told the story of this debt, and how it was a deep spiritual wound for me. During the course of making the film, I continually checked in with the Spirit of Peace through meditation, to receive guidance. I was consistently shown that I should proceed, forwarding the money from my own resources and borrowing as necessary, because the film was important and the money would come. I operated this way, with faith and a rapidly skyrocketing debt load, until I finally realized I could go on no longer.

The lesson I was carrying from that story was some doubt about being able to trust my inner guidance, and bitterness at having this enormous personal debt that I couldn't see how I would ever pay off.

Patricia listened to this tale of woe, and very calmly asked me if I could tell the same story in a different way. Suddenly, things shifted in my mind. Whole chunks of information that I had had all along fell together into a new shape, and I had a completely different story! I realized that, as the film neared completion, I began to get feedback from a variety of sources that the release of this documentary could cause harm. Not only could some individuals be personally hurt, but the potential for certain groups to twist the meaning of the film and use it for their own propaganda would defeat the entire purpose of the project.

Suddenly, I saw I had not been misled at all. On the contrary. When it became clear that the project was no longer a useful contribution, the Spirit of Peace got my attention to shut things down through lack of money. I realized it was far better to carry a financial debt than a karmic one, from the harm I could have caused. This refiguring of how I held the truth of this experience allowed me to accept the debt joyously, as a privilege rather than as a burden. And now, seven years after this new awareness, the debt repayment is nearly completed.

Through the Lens of Our Myths

One of the things I find so powerful about this ability to reframe our stories at will is the understanding that stories told frequently develop into myths. Once a story has reached the stage of myth, it acquires a certain timelessness and a wide range of associations. Events are magnified, heroes and heroines are glorified, enemies are vilified, and the whole thing becomes embedded in our consciousness as a truth central to the definition of our identity.

Awakening the Mind of Peace

Stories that become myths also affect us archetypally, touching our collective consciousness with themes and images that sound a much larger note than the original story by itself. By that time, the story is hard to change, and the actors are captured forever, as in amber, in the acts of legend. Anyone then challenging the myth is seen as challenging the integrity of the individual or the group.

Family myths are a good example of this. In my own family, my mother tells of the time I was born as the origin of the difficult relationship I had with my brother. She reports bringing me home from the hospital and placing me in a bassinet. My three-year-old brother, according to this mythic telling of the story, leaned over the bassinet and said, "Oh, what a pretty baby." Then, POW! His fist shot out for the first blow. She told this story often enough to engrave it in our minds, and did so with humor, as if it were an amusing moment in the family journal.

Since neither my brother nor I remember this incident on our own, my mother's retelling became the myth we lived by. My brother was forever frozen in that moment of jealous rage (and what older sibling has not had the same feeling?), while I was cast indefinitely as the innocent helpless victim. The fact that my brother and I struggled with this set of behaviors and roles throughout our lives was reinforced by the power of the family myth.

Groups too have their myths, and the dynamic is even more powerful on a group level, because it can be used as a means of social control. Anyone who doesn't accept the myth and all its ramifications is a traitor, or internal enemy. Thus, for instance, the mythologizing around the founding of the American nation leans heavily on the glories of the early settlers, the wisdom of the founding fathers, the glorious revolution for freedom from tyranny, the creation of the two timeless documents (the Declaration of Independence and the Constitution), and the taming of the West.

While these stories are indeed inspiring, what's missing from this myth is the devastation these events wrought for the Native Americans, whose lands were taken and cultures destroyed to make way for the new nation, and for the African slaves, on whose backs its economy was brutally built. Yet those who try to include these viewpoints in the history books are charged with being dangerously revisionist, going overboard with political correctness, or, even worse, raising issues that are simply irrelevant.

Our founding myth has taken on a life of its own, and become too powerful to allow for the possibility of multiple truths existing within it. Unfortunately, therefore, a basic wound in our social fabric continues to fester under the skin of this great nation. For the stories we tell ourselves about ourselves have great power to hold the seeds of peace or of conflict for many generations.

Paige Chargois, a minister from Richmond, Virginia, had a story that she had told herself about the Confederate flag all her life. To her, and to many other African Americans, that flag was a particularly odious symbol.

All of my life my parents and the church had taught me to pray to God. For me, honesty, purity, unselfishness, and love were virtually automatic—from the cradle I was taught those qualities by my devout parents and church leaders. I also had role models all around me in whom I could see these virtues not just at work in our family life, but making a difference throughout our community.

Awakening the Mind of Peace

But in these later years, within a less protected environment, the challenge to love has become far more pronounced. A warrior in the civil rights struggle, I thought I had already learned to love. I thought I had overcome any hatred and bitterness toward white people, but the Confederate flag kept coming into my mind. That was something I just couldn't love. It had become a symbol of hatred of southern whites against black people. Within the African American psyche, it suggested our annihilation or our continuing second-class citizenship.

The city in which I live was the capital of the Confederacy, and its flag is still flown from private houses, draped across the window of pickup trucks, and used in myriad ways. No matter when or where I saw it, it inspired a deep sense of hatred in my very being. God was not content for me to live with that hatred, but I didn't know how to free myself from it. As I got involved in Moral Rearmament's 1993 "Hope in the Cities" conference, I knew I had to find a way to move toward what and whom I hated.

I found myself sitting in the living room of a former officer in the United Daughters of the Confederacy, an organization that until recently used the Confederate flag in their organizational logo and on their letterhead. I sat with my back intentionally turned toward her flag, which was sentimentally placed near the photos of her father on the credenza, all the while trying to get over being incensed just by seeing it when I walked into her living room.

A very old lady, she began to tell me her side of the Civil War, including how her father had tried to find homes for black babies and white babies after the war. In the couple of hours we spent together, God said to me that I could not be free of my hatred until I acknowledged and accepted her pain. I listened. God gave the victory!

That has led me to an effort to bring together white leaders of the Confederate persuasion with black leaders for dialogue. This dialogue led to an institutional shift, when the executive director of the Museum of the Confederacy declared that such a place must become a learning center for the whole community, and no longer merely a repository of Civil War artifacts.

I love this story because it shows how opening to another person's pain without denying one's own can ultimately lead to a transformation of the situation to the benefit of both. While Paige learned to encompass a larger set of truths beyond the familiar myths of her identity, many of us do not. The inability to hold multiple truths simultaneously is a powerful hindrance to right relationship. In every situation, each party will have his or her own story of what happened, how it happened, why it happened, who's responsible, and what the effects are. To suppose that only one version of the event can be accurate is to condemn us all to a monochrome existence. Life is far more colorful and intricate than single truths.

We each have the truth of our experience; that is, how we experience something as true for us. In seeing through the lens of our myths, we must learn to reach out for all the truths, and allow ourselves to be enriched rather than threatened by some one else's view.

Through the Lens of Our Wholeness

One of the things that concerns me greatly as I travel around the world is the degree to which we have allowed ourselves to be hypnotized by our political leaders and media. We have given our power away to the popular culture, to the slogans and ideologies of the day, to the mediocre, the mass-produced, the chain store, the sound byte. In doing this, we have become lethargic, de-energized. We go along to get along.

By allowing ourselves to coast in this way, we dumb down, and make ourselves vulnerable to manipulation and control. We forget what is possible. We forget what our potential is. We ignore our own power. The Rwandan massacres and the war in Bosnia are examples of how people allowed their political leadership to lead them past the limits of humanity through this type of hypnosis. In the first dialogue I facilitated in Bosnia between Serbs, Bosniaks, and Croats, one of the most compelling questions that came up was, "Where were the intellectuals? Why were they silent?"

To see each other as we really are, we need to empower ourselves anew, looking beyond the masks we wear, the lethargy of our routine lives and the manipulation of our environment. We need to reach through these obstacles to remember our true nature, so that we can relate to that essential spark of divinity in one another rather than to the surface display.

I once asked two groups of peacebuilders from opposing sides of a bitter ideological conflict to make a skit showing their possibilities for the future. First, they drew a line down the middle of the floor, to indicate the wall of their psychological separation. Then, they mimicked their various political and religious leaders, displaying with grand and expansive gestures the propagandistic harangues they were so regularly subjected to.

While the leaders were pontificating, some people on each side were milling around aimlessly, like animals in a herd. Others sat motionless, in a coma-like state. Suddenly, they realized the wall separating them had somehow disappeared, and all was chaos. How could they relate to each other without that wall? They had no preparation for this, no guidance from their leaders for something so new and unexpected. They had to explore, oh so tentatively, a whole new relationship of their own making.

This poignant scene could well have been staged in any number of places around the world, including in the cities of America. We give up thinking for ourselves and rely on others to tell us how our relationships should be. In doing so, we forget our own potency, our own inherent wisdom, and the wisdom and power of the "other" as well. Then our relationships remain in cycles of reactivity on the surface, within clearly defined borders, and we never have to challenge ourselves to go deeper, to understand more fully, to touch the mystery in one another.

We also give up our opportunity to touch the mystery in ourselves. We forget who we really are, and all the power and possibility that rests in our natural state of divine wholeness.

My brother and I had a great and glorious healing just before he died of cancer at age forty-one. We got to see each other, finally, as we truly are, and all the difficulties in our past slipped away in the light of that clear love.

He was diagnosed with T-cell lymphoma, and all the traditional medical treatments he tried failed to stop the rapid spread of the disease. Though he had witnessed my healing from cancer through non-traditional means some years previously, he was very clear: "I'm a medical doctor," he said. "I'm a scientist. That alternative stuff may have worked for you, but the evidence is all anecdotal. For me, if you can't prove it in the laboratory, I'm not interested." So he chose to undergo an extremely toxic and experimental treatment as a last-ditch effort to save his life. "But you could," he advanced tentatively, "teach me to meditate a little."

Because of the massive hits of radiation required in his treatment, my brother required a bone marrow transplant. I was the donor. He was extremely touched that I would make that offering and go through that operation for him.

With that mind set, we entered the hospital together. He would receive massive doses of radiation in an attempt to kill all the cancer cells. It would, of course, also destroy the viability of his bone marrow and totally deplete his immune system. My bone marrow would then be harvested and transplanted to him, in the hopes that it would engraft in him and grow him back a healthy immune system.

Since the hospital was in a city far from my home, I needed to leave fourteen days after my part of the surgery, but I didn't want to leave before knowing that the transplant had taken hold. It normally takes several weeks for the new bone marrow to fully engraft, and since we didn't want to wait that long, we made an agreement. We would meditate together to bring on the engrafting by day thirteen, so I could leave the following day with peace of mind for both of us.

Our strategy was simple. As a doctor, he knew what these cells looked like, what the chemical and biological processes were as the marrow began to take hold and grow. As a meditation practitioner, I knew how to see and hold him in his inherent state of perfect wellness. So every day, we sat together and did this meditation, he visualizing the cellular activity and I calling forth the light of his perfection.

Meeting each other in this pure place of light and love, all vestiges of our painful history dissolved, and we spent those two weeks in a state of true brother/sister grace.

Every day the nurse would test his blood. On day thirteen, our target date, she came back into the room in confusion. "I'm sorry, Dr. Hantman," she said. "There's been some mistake with your blood work. The tests showed you've engrafted from the transplant, but we know that's not medically possible, so we'll have to run the test again." My brother and I glanced at each other conspiratorially, happy to let them draw more blood. We already knew the outcome. Sure enough, he did engraft on the thirteenth day, just as we had intended.

"I tried to kill you," he said, "and you saved my life." As we embraced in that moment, the healing was complete, at every level.

My brother died a month later, from an upsurge of the cancer. He had a fully functioning immune system at the time. Though he was not cured of the cancer, he was healed of his spiritual malady. He died at peace, having transformed his greatest "enemy" into his loving ally. This would not have been possible if both of us had not been able to reach beneath the surface into the very depths of one another's souls, and find the beauty and love just waiting to spill from that place.

Awakening the Mind of Peace: Meeting in the Light

Living in right relationship is an ongoing journey. We slip out of the stream of right relationship again and again, building up that mountain of lies rather than tearing it down. We will slip out of the stream over and over, and need to gently bring ourselves back to focus on what is true. We breathe in: We are all related. We breathe out: We need to care for one another.

We can speed this remembering if at least one party in the relationship moves beyond the normal, accustomed way of relating and slips into a new perspective. We could say that this new perspective comes from our higher self. That is, when we remember some aspect of our own true and perfect nature, or can touch the holy spark in the other, everything changes. This is called "meeting in the light."

We have learned to live in a fog. That fog obscures the sacred light of who and what we really are, and how we are indelibly connected. Every so often, the clouds part, and we are startled by the brightness of the sun. Everything is shining and glorious for that one brief moment. Then the fog rolls in again.

This fog is our own separative mind that cannot see the whole for seeing the parts. It tricks us, as individuals and as groups, into believing we are alone. It shrouds the reality of our interconnectedness, and the possibility of working together for common solutions to our shared problems. In the dimness of this fog, we see our own shadows in those around us, and then live in fear of the demons we imagine lurking in the mists.

Our task, like that of my brother and of Paige Chargois, the African American woman who chose to listen to the Confederate woman, is to cut through the fog to find the place of divine light, and to manage our relationships from that place. We need to meet the light in ourselves and in each other, and we need to hold whatever happens between us as an aspect of that light seeking to brighten itself. Like centering home, this is a lifetime practice.

We can choose, over and over again, to remember our connection to all life forms, and deepen our subtle communication with those around us. We can make a conscious choice to act for the highest quality and purpose of every relationship, seeing each as an opportunity for our mutual learning and spiritual growth. We can stay through the hard times, committed to finding ways to honor each other in new forms of partnership.

Facing into our pain, reframing how we think about one another, telling our stories in a different way, and relating to the inherent wholeness that is our birthright—these are avenues for seeing each other as we really are. We can also discard our victim and villain masks, and reintegrate what we have polarized and projected by finding ourselves in the other.

As I write these words, I am reminded of the heartwarming hospitality I have received in countless settings all over the United States and around the world. I have been welcomed, fed, and lovingly tended by farmers in Appalachia, fishermen in Scotland, cave dwellers in India, and Native American elders in Arizona. I have been hosted at an elaborate banquet in Taiwan, at a simple meal of bread and olives in a refugee camp, and at a religious feast in Greece.

I am also reminded that many religious traditions teach us to treat with generosity the stranger at our door. I find in this reflection on hospitality to strangers a double message about the practice of right relationship. First, in that everyday reality where our rich diversity makes us appear strange to each other, when we make a warm place for those differences at our hearth, no matter how high or humble, we are recognizing ourselves in each other.

At the higher level, in that larger reality where our relatedness simply is, there is no such thing as a stranger. In that place, these acts of kindness are ways we acknowledge that we do indeed belong to each other. We care for one another as we ourselves would like to be cared for, not because we want to get what we give, but because in honoring the guest we honor the one that we are.

When I center home, I find the hope of peace. When I meet all my relations in the light, knowing that we are inseparable, I rediscover the mind of peace. In this way, the Spirit of Peace awakens, and invites us to the dance floor, where we might dance our knowing of right relationship, for the benefit of all our relations.

Practice Meeting in the Light

The following exercises give us a direct experience of our interconnectedness and belonging. They invite us to develop the skills of reframing and reowning projections so that we can increase our capacity for right relationship.

1. Meditative Practice for Meeting in the Light

Begin, as before, by sitting comfortably, aligning yourself and centering home with the breath. When you have found that deep place of Peace within, think of someone with whom you have a difficult relationship, someone toward whom you may have unresolved negative feelings. Imagine this person in front of you. Drawing on your inner resources, send the person a message of gratitude for all the opportunities they are providing for you to grow in your understanding of right relationship. Let them know what you value about this relationship, and what you are learning and still hope to learn. Acknowledge them as a relative in the family of life, and greet the inherent wisdom potential within them. Breathe into this experience. What do you notice?

2. Action Practice for Meeting in the Light

Again, think of someone with whom you have a difficult relationship. On a piece of paper, write down a series of statements that describe that person, using the "you" form. (Example: You are selfish and never think about my needs.) Now go back through the list and read each statement in the first person, as if it were about yourself. (Example: I am selfish and never think about your needs.) Read the new statement slowly, and sit with it for a moment. To what extent is it true? What have you learned about yourself and this relationship through this exercise?

THREE

We are broken
And we will not be mended
Until we remember
That we are unbreakable.

Opening the Heart of Peace

The Power of Love

CHARLOTTE WAS A Swiss woman who made the decision during World War II to work with the French Resistance. She was aware of the risks, realizing that capture would not only mean the end of her usefulness, but would most certainly involve being tortured for information, and, if she survived that, the inevitable transport to a concentration camp.

Nonetheless, Charlotte persevered. She served the Resistance in various capacities for four years. Finally, she was caught. Jailed by the Gestapo, Charlotte awaited her interrogation with great trepidation. When she was escorted into the interrogation chamber, however, Charlotte found herself in a most improbable state. Her heart suddenly opened, and she began viewing her captors with great love! She felt a pure radiance shining through her to the men who would surely deal viciously with her. She said nothing, simply relaxing into that state of love.

Inexplicably, whenever her tormentors would begin to question her, something odd would happen. A phone call or summons would come that would call them away, or some other outside force would stop the interrogation before it could complete its course. Even when she was put on the train for the camps, the train didn't run. Charlotte, choosing to stay in a state of love rather than of fear, even in the most violent of circumstances, escaped the worst of the harm that could have befallen her.

Spiritual Lesson 3
Love Is the Glue That Can Mend What Is Broken

So far I have posited two basic spiritual principles: We are one, and in that oneness, we are all related. Now it's time to look at what keeps us connected in that vast web of interrelationships. I suggest that the glue that holds the universe together, that binds us in our belonging to one another and is the very substance of our wholeness and our holiness, is love.

Just like the drop of water in the larger ocean, so too does love exist in various dimensions simultaneously. At the personal level, we feel love for those close to us, our families and our friends. At the metaphysical level, love is impersonal and universal, available to all equally. At the personal level, we try to constrain and condition our love in many ways. "I will love you if. . ." and its corollary, "If you really loved me, you would. . ." form the subtext, often subliminal, of many a relationship. At the spiritual level, love is unconditional and unbounded, an endless outpouring of divine caring of creation and created for one another, without regard to any limiting factor.

To understand the power of love on a cosmic level we have to go back to the basic question of creation: How did the world as we know it come into being? Every culture has its own version of an answer to this primal question, and these various answers set in motion whole belief systems that define different civilizations on the planet and affect how we live our everyday lives.

I am not a scholar, and am unable to compare and contrast the creation stories of many cultures to look for common elements. Nor am I a scientist who can correlate the essential truths of those myths with the currently available scientific data. I am a simple human being who has, like many others, faced into the dark and starry night sky with wonder and awe, and asked, How and why?

The best answer I have come up with goes something like this: In the beginning is a vast, all-encompassing, and ultimately ineffable Beingness that unfolds itself continuously, through infinite potential, into form: the One, undifferentiated, unexpressed, unarticulated. That One seeks to know itself in its myriad possibilities, and in that act of manifesting itself, now two aspects of the One exist: the creator and the created. This is not a process that happened once, a long time ago, but is continually occurring in an ongoing process of creation.

Once there are two, there are also three—the creator, the created, and the relationship or energy between them. As the two are inherently inseparable, two forms of the same essence, the link between them is unending and unbreakable; the created arising from and returning to its source, even as the out-breath leaves the body to go out into the world, but ultimately returns as the in-breath, carrying new energy and information with it. That desire to know itself that characterizes the One, and the desire to return to its Source that characterizes each element of creation, is the attraction force that holds creation together. We experience it in many forms, and call it love.

Religions throughout the ages have attempted to interpret their own version of the phenomenon of creation. The Judeo-Christian faith traditions speak of God as an all-loving father, who created the world in his image. It posits love as our divine inheritance, and as the primary spiritual law of human interaction, as in the commandments: "Thou shalt love thy neighbor as thyself" and "Thou shalt love the Lord thy God with all thy heart, with all thy soul, and with all thy might." Other religions that may not be organized around the concept of a personal God still speak about the importance of compassion, caring, and loving kindness as our spiritual heritage, birthright, and duty.

Bringing this back to everyday realities, we know from our own experience that love expands and enlivens us. When our hearts are open, love flows like a fountain of goodness and blessing. When we feel love for another—a family member, a friend, a beloved partner—and feel their love for us, our senses are heightened and our vibrancy increased. All is right with the world. We are happy.

The deeper and fuller the love we feel, the more we know that connection, that oneness, that blending or joining of energies. This is why marriage is considered a sacred union—we become one in our love. Love is the magnetic force of attraction that draws us into the core of one another, where our own individuality dissolves momentarily into the greater force field and transcendence of our union.

Conversely, when we are not in the stream of love, we feel lonely, isolated, afraid. We tighten up, exhibit shallow breathing, feel less vibrancy. When our love flow is closed down, we are literally heavy-hearted. Life appears more difficult; we feel the burden of our bitterness and pain. We may feel needy or cynical, angry, or depressed. We are apart from, not a part of, those around us.

All of this confirms for me that love is our natural state. I experience it as a river or stream that, fed by the waters of life, never stops flowing. My choice is to jump into the stream and allow myself to go with it, or to stand on the bank and watch it go by. Once in the stream, I also have choices. I can push against the flow, stay safely in the shallow waters, or surrender myself to the deepest channel, where the current will carry me through myriad landscapes and experiences.

Given these assumptions—that love is the spiritual attractive power of creation and is always available to us in boundless measure—I find that my spiritual evolution consists of developing an ever-greater capacity for living with an open heart. This is not always easy, but then, if it were easy, that would mean we had mastered this lesson and could move on to another. For myself personally, and for the human family in general, I think we still have a long way to go.

What Is Reconciliation?

Reconciliation is the natural process of setting things right again in our relationships. It is more than making up after a fight. It is about remembering that we belong to each other, and clearing whatever gets in the way of living that knowing.

We are all in need of reconciliation. No one I know has escaped life without the scars of a broken heart or the wounds of a soured relationship. Our friends and loved ones treat us in ways that bring pain. We feel rejected, unloved, or misunderstood; we have been abandoned, betrayed, or abused. We ache from all the moments in our lives when our loving nature was denied, our specialness demeaned, or some aspect of our being pronounced "not enough" or "too much" by those whose esteem and acceptance we sought.

At the same time, we are also the agents of hurt for others. Who among us hasn't spoken a cross or scornful word that we later regretted, or treated another in an unfeeling or even cruel way? Who among us has not turned our love away from those close to us, in pique or in self-protection, in selfishness or in laziness, or from fear of intimacy? We have all had moments in our lives when we have hardened our hearts toward others.

Not yet masters of right relationship, we all participate in relationships that are less than fully loving, where hurt happens and people are wounded. In addition, we all belong to groups whose current or historical relationships with other groups are in need of resolution and healing. This is the great educational laboratory of human relations: that we rub up against one another with all our differences, and are challenged to find ways to live and work together without generating harm. As a species, we are still in the early grades of this school. As individuals, we are each in charge of our own advancement.

The word *reconciliation* itself tells us that the process is continuous or repetitive—to "re"-concile is to bring again to resolution. This suggests that right relationship is a dynamic state, not a static, fixed one. We move in and out of harmony with one another. As with meditation, when we notice our mind has wandered from its attention to the breath, so with reconciliation, we notice when a relationship is out of harmony and, as gently as possible, bring ourselves back to balance.

Reconciliation is a complex phenomenon that poses a variety of challenges and opportunities for our spiritual development: How can we heal from a broken heart, or a broken spirit? How and when do we forgive ourselves and others? Is it possible to forgive but not forget? Are there some wounds too deep to heal? Of what value is apology? Can we rebuild trust after betrayal? What is beyond blame? Is restitution needed, and if so, in what form?

The Magic of Love

If our challenge is to live with an open heart, in our natural state of love, then we need to find ways of clearing the obstacles that impede the free flowing of that stream. We do not need to "make" love; love already is. Rather, we need to know and access love, to amplify and express it. In order to do that, we may need to let love lift us beyond our fear (for surely fear, not hatred, is the true opposite of love), and work its transformative magic in our hearts and in our lives.

I know a very special peacebuilder whose story demonstrates the power of love to change a situation. Patrick lives in Kenya, a country that has known recurring cycles of ethnic violence over the years. I was working with a group of peacebuilders that included Patrick, demonstrating how the energy of our thoughts shape our reality. For a while, the group members were on the edge of their chairs with interest. Then, suddenly, they sat back and there was a deep silence. I wasn't sure what the silence meant, nor what, if anything, I should do about it.

After a bit, a wise woman spoke up and said, "You know, we are simple Christian people here, and we tend to think that if there is something we don't understand, it must either be from God or the Devil. My guess is, in this silence, we are trying to figure out which one this is." I was even more taken aback. If they decided that what I was teaching—and therefore I myself—were from the Devil, what might happen? I had the thought to say, "How about if the power or energy we are talking about here is the energy of love?"

This was followed by a second silence, in which I felt much was hanging in the balance. Then Patrick spoke up. He told about the torture he had endured as a political prisoner in his country's jail cells. He said the only way he was able to survive it with his soul intact (though his body was permanently damaged) was to remember the power of love, especially his love of God and God's love for him. His sharing of this story opened the floodgates, and soon other stories were pouring out, about how people had overcome fear, violence, and hatred through the power of love.

Patrick told me later that day that, though the torture had happened many years previously, this was the first time he had spoken of it publicly. Recently, some years after our workshop, he told me that this event had been a turning point for him, allowing him to write a book about his prison experiences and release himself from the constant fear tied up in the past.

Mending the Sacred Hoop

The Native American worldview has a concept that helps me better understand reconciliation and the transforming power of love. It speaks of the oneness of life as a sacred circle, in which all living beings exist together in balance and harmony. In the circle, no one is above or below; no one is better than or worse than another. No one has the right to dominate, control, or demean another. All are part of the same sacred hoop of life, and as such deserve respect, appreciation, and love.

When that hoop has been broken, when one individual or group has aggressed against another in some way, love has been denied or restricted. To restore the flow, we must mend what is broken, realizing that the natural state is the wholeness of the circle. To mend the hoop is to restore right relationship, recalling our intrinsic oneness, and allowing once again the natural power of love to thrive. I believe this is the spiritual challenge of humanity at this time in our evolution, and therefore a daily opportunity for each of us.

Mending the sacred hoop happens in many ways. Essentially, there are three processes involved: (1) We need to stop the behavior that creates the harm; (2) we need to start doing new behaviors that will engender harmony; and (3) we need to clean up the mess resulting from the past harmful behavior, whether our own or others. In order to do this, we must face directly into our own pain, finding ways to heal and transmute it. We must acknowledge the harmful effects of our actions on others and make amends, and, finally, we must deal compassionately with the suffering of others.

The Forgiveness Spectrum

Forgiveness by itself is not all there is to reconciliation. Nor is forgiveness alone the whole of healing. It is only one piece, the part that has to do with changing our own hearts. I like to think of forgiveness as a giving over, a giving up, or giving away of what I am holding onto that hardens my heart, whether that is anger, fear, blame, shame, sorrow, or bitterness. Whatever another person may have done to me, or not done for me, I am the one who has to live with the resulting damage, so my job is to find a way to reopen my heart channel.

Indeed, because of this need to address the flow of love in my life, I might even think of the hurt I suffer as an opportunity for spiritual growth. In Buddhist philosophy, it is said that our greatest enemy is our greatest teacher, to whom we should feel gratitude, for it is by their presence in our lives that we are able to learn our spiritual lessons. If love is the cosmic glue and the path of evolution, then every opportunity I have to increase love in my life and in the world and to transform the countless obstacles in its path must be a blessing.

Though most of our major religions enjoin us to forgive those who have hurt us, it is neither an easy nor a simple task. In fact, the subject of forgiveness is quite complex. What is forgiveness? Does it mean we no longer feel pain, bitterness, and loss? Does it mean we release the one who has hurt us from the consequences of their behavior? When do we need to forgive ourselves, and are there circumstances in which forgiveness is either not possible or not appropriate? Do we have any responsibility for the harm that befalls us?

As each of us struggles with these questions, one thing is clear. Forgiveness is something that happens inside us, regardless of whether the perpetrator of the hurt has apologized, shown remorse, made amends, or not. Forgiveness is an internal process we go through, of feeling our pain, grieving our losses, releasing the bitterness, healing the wound, extracting the lessons, pardoning (not excusing) the perpetrator, and moving on.

This process unfolds over time, in various stages that can not be programmed but arise from a natural progression of each individual's unique experience. While there is no magic formula for reaching a state of forgiveness, there are certain common elements of the process we might consider. These have to do with rebuilding trust, completing our mourning, forgoing revenge, seeking rituals to assist our change of heart, and being open to the grace and power of love so the Spirit of Peace can move in us.

When Trust Is Betrayed

Trust is a delicate thing. Some of us feel safe in the world, and trust others easily; some of us do not. Probably all of us, at one time or another, have had our trust betrayed or broken by one we hold dear. It can happen through an unfeeling word, spoken casually; it can happen through an act of cruelty or selfishness; it can happen through a repeated pattern of behavior that sends the message that we are not respected, appreciated, or loved.

When we hold a reasonable belief that we will be treated respectfully, and then we are treated instead in a way that violates that confidence, the fragile threads of trust may fray or break altogether. If this happens with one person, we need reweave those strands of trust in the relationship. If it happens to us repeatedly, from different directions, we may begin to feel unsafe in our world, or in a particular environment, or with a particular group of people, and then our search for building trust is a harder one.

Trust is a complex phenomenon with several aspects. First and foremost is a sense of safety: I need to trust that I will not come to harm in a particular relationship. Next is a sense of being understood: I need to know that the other knows what is important to me, and will honor that. Next is a sense of caring: I need to know that the other cares enough about me to want to understand what's important to me, and to treat me accordingly, even at the risk of some sacrifice on their part.

The sense of solidarity is also important: I need to know that the other will stand up for me in difficult times, will be my personal cheerleader and supporter. Finally is the sense of trustworthiness: I need to know that the other will tell me the truth, do what they say they will do, and fulfill their commitments to me.

Sonja, a teacher in New York City, tells of a time in her life when all these terms of trust were broken, and of the inner work she had to do to reestablish trust.

— Six years ago I met the love of my life. I didn't know it at first. In fact, my first impression of the man was not so great. But the setting was wildly exciting and romantic—I was abroad, studying and traveling. Roberto and I met and spent all of our free time together.

After I left, we decided to try to maintain a long-distance primary relationship. We would rendezvous in Europe or in the States for long weekends, vacations, or any opportunity we could create. In these very short, very intense times together, our love grew deeper.

Then, one time while I was visiting Roberto in Italy, I happened to come across some information that made it very clear I was not the only woman in his life. I was shocked and devastated. I didn't know what to think or how to handle it. We talked it through, and in the end I let myself explain away his behavior. It must be due to the long distance between us, and all of our differences, plus the short time we had been together, I reasoned.

We stayed together. I even moved to Italy to live with him. It happened again, and again. I left him, he fought for me, I left him again, and again returned. It was a vicious cycle. Finally I left for good. I returned to the States to start a new life. I literally had to start from scratch—job, home, everything. It was the hardest thing I ever did, but I succeeded, and proved to myself my own capabilities.

But still I struggled with depression and loneliness. I sought therapy and leaned very heavily on my mother and my other friends. I had to look very deep inside myself and, without blaming myself for his actions, I had to face my own fears and weaknesses. My anger and frustration were eating me alive, and I had to find a release.

One suggestion that my therapist recommended turned out to be my breakthrough. I took strips of paper and wrote down all of my feelings about Roberto, my situation, myself—anger, frustration, guilt, sadness, emptiness, hate, rage, worthlessness—everything. Then I set each piece of paper on fire, one by one, and watched as they disappeared into thin air. It was so satisfying, letting go and releasing, that I did it again. I felt a great sense of lightness and relief—I felt free!

Soon after that, Roberto came back again, literally knocking on my door. I wasn't ready to see him or talk to him, but we started being in contact again. He called me from Europe every day. I was in such a different place with myself and with what had happened that I was able to talk to him as I had never been able to before. I told him exactly what I thought about him, about us, about what he had and hadn't done. Our communication was better than it had ever been. I had absolutely nothing to lose with him, because I was no longer attached to the bitterness and distrust, or to the expectations.

The more we talked things through, the more we both realized that we still had a deep connection and caring for one another. It took many months until I was ready to see him again, but we did eventually get back together and we are happily married today.

What really made that possible? The process I went through to reestablish trust wasn't at all easy. Most of my family and friends were very opposed to our reunion, and who could blame them, since they had seen him hurt me time and again, and had been there to pick up the pieces? Of course they wondered how I could ever trust him again, and why I would put myself in a position to risk being hurt again.

The way I dealt with the issue of trust was, over time, to learn to trust myself. I knew that I still loved this man, I knew that our time together was not finished. I had to trust those feelings. Did I know he was never going to cheat on me again? No. But he proved to me in the time we were working our way back to each other that he wanted so much to be able to look in the mirror again and be proud of himself. He wanted the opportunity to prove his love and fidelity. I can't explain what his personal journey was like, but I do believe he went through as much soul searching as I did in our time apart.

The process was hard and long, and every step of the way those old fears and feelings kept creeping back. What's different for me is that I don't let them control me anymore. I realized that I want to be with him, and that we couldn't be together if I held on to those fears. I had learned that the closer I held them to me, the more they only hurt and hindered me. So I let them go, and I decided to follow my heart and take a leap of faith. I don't regret it at all.

In my international work of peacebuilding, I am often in places where trust is virtually nonexistent between conflicting parties. People fully expect that the other will try to hurt them. They do not believe any promises made, and simply assume that the "enemy" will take advantage of every situation for their own benefit. They may even assume that they are in physical danger any time they are near someone from the other group. I remember specifically one man who attended a meeting involving people from both sides of the conflict he was involved in. Sharing a hotel suite with someone from the other side, he was very careful to lock the door leading from his bedroom to the common living room, lest the enemy in the next room decide to come for him in the night.

In these settings, trust needs to be built slowly, step by step, and even when people have learned to trust one another, the slightest mishap may catapult the relationship right back to where it started. Distrust has become the default setting of the system, and acts powerfully to pull people back into its false promise of protection.

I remember a time in an Eastern European country where peace-builders from two groups with a long history as deadly enemies met for the first time to discuss their situation. The level of distrust was high. As part of the dialogue, we looked together at the history of the conflict, and each side had a chance to present their version of the history. Afterwards, there was a stunned silence. I asked what was happening. One participant replied, "They lied to us. All our lives, our leaders, parents, and teachers told us the history only from our point of view. We never knew there was another way to look at it."

The realization that they had all been victims of broken trust was, paradoxically, the beginning of the development of trust among the participants. They were able to work together to improve understanding, building confidence in each other and in the possibilities for peace as they did so.

While trust alone is not sufficient to induce forgiveness, it is a necessary element in the forgiveness spectrum. In fact, we may be able to forgive without having yet developed the necessary trust to rebuild and heal the relationship. However, taking the risk to trust, stepping out along that path even tentatively, is a critical first step.

Completing Our Mourning

When we have been hurt, there is usually some loss involved. If another person has treated us badly, we may have lost our sense of safety with him or her, or perhaps the relationship is lost to us altogether. We may have lost our desire to stay connected, or our belief in ourselves as a loving and lovable person. In extreme situations, we may actually lose our loved ones, our jobs, or our homes.

When there is loss, there is both grief and anger. These two emotions are the flip side of one another. Some of us are more comfortable expressing the sadness, others the anger. Both are usually present when we have suffered harm, and both must be addressed if we are to complete our mourning.

As human beings we have developed infinite ways to avoid mourning. Instead we keep our loss alive and festering by maintaining a righteous stance, pointing the finger of blame at the one who hurt us and holding ourselves in the victim role. Or we adopt a stiff upper lip approach, and carry on after a wound as if everything were OK, denying the reality of our pain.

Neither of these activities helps reopen our heart stream. Instead, they act like fat in our arteries, damming up the flow of love's course. To come to a place of forgiveness, we need to deal both with the anger and the pain of loss. Depending on the depth of the hurt and our emotional skills, this is likely to be a process that happens over time.

Janet Evergreen, a healing practitioner in Charlottesville, Virginia, tells of a time her young son allowed himself to go deeply into mourning over the loss of his birth mother. Because of her own painful childhood, Janet decided at age twelve to become an advocate for troubled children. She and her husband became an emergency foster placement family for eighty children over several years. During this time, they also had a biological daughter, and adopted two sons with attachment disorders and learning disabilities. Managing all this was a great challenge.

Opening the Heart of Peace

One time I was alone with the children, and they were being very demanding. I knew they each needed my attention and I had to keep going just to get the chores done. Suddenly, there was a fight between the boys. Each was hurt, each entrenched in patterns of loss. My little girl needed someone to reassure her that our home was still safe. I felt in a lose/lose situation. If I turned my attention to one of my three children, I would be repeating an instance of abandonment with the others. I felt frustrated and overwhelmed; my hope of creating a loving, safe, and happy home seemed unrealistic.

Just then our friend Kristen arrived and without missing a beat, she offered to do the chores and take care of two of the children. I took my three-year-old son upstairs to be alone with me. He was still crying. I prayed for guidance. I sat and rocked him in the rocking chair for a long time. Suddenly, we were in a timeless place, his crying no longer about the fight with his brother.

He traveled from this grief to the grief of adoption with us, the foster homes before us, the separation from his birth mother, the difficult times while in her care. His sobs racked his body. I covered him with an old shirt and just held him close, to hold the grief for him until he was ready to let go. Leaning into the arms of the Spirit of Peace, I was held and given the strength to be quiet and present, to ride the wave of energy flowing from my new son.

In time the sobbing stopped. He shivered and shook one last time and took a new breath. He poked his head through the top of the covering. He said, "I'm all better," smiled, and hopped down to go play. It was as if down in the warm darkness, next to my belly, he rebirthed himself, and I felt for the first time bonded to him and to his life's journey.

Like this young boy, all of us feel loss, though we may not acknowledge it. Indeed, the denial of loss can be, literally, a deadly phenomenon. Millions of people around the world have become refugees as a result of war and aggression in the last half-century. Whole villages, clans, and families have lost their homes and possessions, their land and livelihoods, and in many cases loved ones as well, through the violence that drove them into refugee camps or to crowded temporary housing in cities or forests, mountain refuges, deserts, or open fields.

Over the years, these refugees or displaced people have had to start all over again, finding new housing, new ways to provide for themselves, often in another country altogether. Always they keep the flame burning of return. They dream of their lost homes, their land. Politically, they hold the right to return as a standard of justice, insisting that it be part of any peace negotiation, while at the same time using the injustice as a rallying point for political and nationalistic fervor.

I have worked in many such settings. While some refugees do go home eventually, the sad truth is that most will not ever see their original homes again. Their villages may have been destroyed. Their houses may be inhabited by other families, who themselves have nowhere else to go. Even if, by some miracle, the refugees could return to their homes, after thirty, forty, or even fifty years or more, things would not be the same as they were.

In these scenarios, people's losses are often not acknowledged as real. Enmeshed and confused with the injustice of the circumstances, they are never fully mourned. Memories are frozen in time, and around those memories grow whole mythologies of victimhood and eternal enmity that are passed on from generation to generation, fueling a

Opening the Heart of Peace

continuing cycle of violence and hatred. Incomplete mourning ensures there will be no forgiveness.

While this example relates to places like the Balkans, the Middle East, and the Horn of Africa, it is also a metaphor for what happens to many of us in our daily lives. Conditions change; the impermanence of life shows itself in many ways. We may have lost a job or a relationship, and instead of grieving that loss, we bemoan our fate, blame others, or carry ourselves as the victims of circumstance, cruelty, or injustice. Like refugees, when we hold on to how things once were, or might have been, without grieving our losses, we make the possibility of forgiveness and reconciliation that much harder.

I Can Forgive but I Can't Forget

There is a subtle line between accepting and acquiescing. Acknowledging loss does not mean condoning the behavior that precipitated it, nor does it mean collapsing into a state of silent acceptance of whatever happens, or giving up our right to seek justice. Sometimes, what others do to us is so awful, so abusive or painful, that we're not sure if we can or should forgive. We do know we can never forget.

This is especially so in circumstances of deep trauma. Again, it would be easy to project this far away from us, and consider such events as the Holocaust in Europe, the killing fields of Cambodia, or the massacres in Rwanda as situations of trauma where we can understand this distinction between forgiving and forgetting. Forgetting what happened in these settings means missing the opportunity to learn from history. It means not holding people accountable for the damage they did to others. Indeed, the very act of remembrance and the commitment to not allow such things to happen again can be an important part of the healing process.

Trauma, however, is not reserved only for the obvious hot spots of the world. The truth is, many of us who live comfortably in Western democracies that are not at war have also been traumatized. In our families, schools, and streets there is much violence, both physical and emotional. All too many of us have been sexually abused, incested, or molested. We may have been deeply hurt by incidents of racial, religious, or ethnic hatred and prejudice.

When we are traumatized, however it may happen, we each face our own road of healing and forgiveness, two different but related processes that unfold over time, each at its own pace. I think, for instance, of peacebuilders I know in Bosnia, who, two and three years after the end of the war there, were only just beginning to tell their stories and feel their feelings about what happened to them. For them, the healing process is just beginning; forgiveness is still in the future.

My relationship with my brother is another example. Though we arrived at a place of complete reconciliation before he died, nonetheless the memory traces of the ways I learned to live with and respond to the hurting part of that relationship still exist for me. My body remembers, and still flinches at sudden or threatening sounds. My heart remembers, and still anticipates the next blow, even when love is being offered. My mind remembers, and still holds fleeting thoughts of being somehow at fault or inherently unlovable.

However long the healing may take, and whatever it may look like for each of us, there are things that can help us along the way. Ritual, grace, and the commitment to transcend revenge are some of these tools.

Opening the Heart of Peace

The Spirit of Peace at the Gates of Hell

The Holocaust is one of those absolutely horrific situations that has fostered intergenerational trauma so deep that some people believe it to be beyond the reach of healing and forgiveness. While dialogues, support groups, and other traditional means of healing have been valuable in gradually relieving the trauma of many whose lives were directly affected by the Holocaust, this is the type of situation well suited to healing rituals.

Rituals give us some distance from the pain, while at the same time creating safe space within which we can experience that pain fully. They provide an orderly and organized channel for transmuting the pain, and are a way to relive and release a traumatic event, while offering it into the keeping of a larger force. In healing rituals, whether done individually or with a group, we transform the energy, literally changing it from one form to another.

Rituals for forgiveness and healing are found in ceremonies or customs of many cultures. For instance, the atonement ritual in the Yom Kippur liturgy for Jews guides an entire religious community in a yearly process of purification and renewal. In the Arab world, particularly in Lebanon, Palestine, and Jordan, the process of *Sulha* is a ritualized way of resolving disputes through the mediation of respected elders, the determination of restitution, and the sealing of the agreement with a joint meal or other public ritual, such as handshaking or public apology.

In the Navajo culture, there are elaborate healing ceremonies that help people come back to right relationship with the sacred circle of life. In Sierra Leone, villages have successfully used local traditional rituals for integrating back into community life those child soldiers who fought and committed atrocities during the civil war.

Rituals can be crafted by individuals or groups to address particular circumstances. Whether traditional or modern, rituals usually rely on certain common elements: they use symbols that are meaningful to the participants; they may use special and repeated sounds or movements that evoke a particular quality of consciousness; they seek to cleanse or release the energy of the trauma; and they usually invoke forces larger than the individual to assist in this process—often communal or spiritual forces.

Paula Green, a professional peacebuilder from Leverett, Massachusetts, writes of such a ritual that she helped create. At the request of the Japanese Buddhist Order Nipponzan Myohoji, she designed and directed a special Convocation of people of all faiths at Auschwitz in 1995.

"How can you speak of being peaceful and loving?" a Jewish woman cries out in anguish to a Quaker fellow-participant during this Convocation. "What do you expect me to do with my rage and anger? It is not time yet for dialogue and understanding."

Two hundred of us are gathered at the International Center in Oswiecim, Poland, a conference center built by the German organization Action-Reconciliation. Half of us will begin the 1995 eight-month peacewalk from Auschwitz to Hiroshima, led by the Japanese Buddhist Nipponzan Myohoji peacewalking order. We gather from the four corners of the Earth for a week of interfaith spiritual dialogue at Auschwitz, risking our souls and sanity here at the gates of hell. We are Christian, Jewish, and Buddhist; German and Japanese; North and South American; European, Asian, and African. We are Cambodians, Native Americans, Bosnians, Guatemalans: so many whose countries have been shattered by hatred before and since the Holocaust.

Among us are spiritual leaders: rabbis, monks, nuns, ministers, and priests who have responded to special invitations to hold the energy and guide the depth of this assembled polyglot community. None of us can imagine the magnitude of Auschwitz, nor how the Convocation will unfold.

We discover an unanticipated blessing: the first day of our gathering is the last night of Hanukkah, the Jewish festival commemorating a miracle of light. Participants fashion rudimentary menorahs, holders for the candles of Hanukkah. We are still largely strangers to one another. Night falls. We form a procession, one by one, silently walking through the darkened streets of Oswiecim to the main gate of Auschwitz, candles and menorahs in the hands of Germans, Japanese, American Jews, rabbis, priests, and monks. We gather around our spiritual teachers and the snow begins to fall, touching our faces like tears. Wordless melodies break the silence, chants to the Spirit of Peace. Candles lit, prayers offered in many tongues, Convocation participants stare at the darkened gates, preparing for this week of dialogue and for our entry into the abyss of Auschwitz and Birkenau.

That authentic and anguished exchange between Jew and Quaker shatters the strained peace of our first dialogue day. Four more days follow, including heart-wrenching witness within the concentration camps. I notice how the community builds, how participants cling to each other across lines of religion and ethnicity, how the dialogues become genuine, how deeply we experience stories from Bosnia, drumming from Native America, slides from Cambodia. We bear witness to Germans whose families participated in the atrocities of Auschwitz and to Jews whose families fell victim to those crimes. At Birkenau, a Christian man from the United States named John falls to his knees, asking repentance. Bina, an elderly Jewish English woman, lights a candle at the crematorium for her father who perished here, finally coming to terms with her father's history so late in her life.

We sit at the train tracks at Birkenau in this cold Polish December with the monks and nuns of Nipponzan Myohoji, who engage in a weeklong prayer vigil and fast on the tracks. Father Herbert, a Pax Christi priest from Germany, holds a portrait of a weeping Christ and tells us about his father's Nazi past. Tears freeze on his cheeks while he speaks. When the tension in the dialogue becomes unbearable, the chanting of Julius, an African American Jew, author, scholar, and musician rises to inspirit the pain, followed by the haunting flute of Father Herbert.

Miracle follows miracle. Helga, a German woman whose father was responsible for the liquidation of a large Polish Jewish community, discovers that Jim, one of our spiritual leaders, is a descendant of that community, in which his relatives perished. Jim and Helga bond, recognizing the twisted fate that brings them together.

Father Yoshida, a Christian priest from Japan, shouts out every day to wake us up to our true reality: "I am Muslim, I am Jewish, I am Buddhist. The time is NOW." Dan, a teacher from the United States, sobs as he places poems of peace written by his students on the display tables of discarded baby clothes at Auschwitz. Claude, an American Vietnam veteran, stares at the guard towers at Birkenau, identifying with the soldiers under orders to commit murder, remembering his own deeds, seeking repentance and personal healing.

The Spirit of Peace holds us together; we could not have survived without her presence. In our final evening, Rabbi Sheila and Father Herbert, American and German, Jew and Christian, join hands and lead the community in sacred dance, transmuting the fires of hatred, acknowledging the presence of genuine relationship, and transforming our differences, our anguish and our tears, for just this moment, in an affirmation of shared humanity.

In the morning, one hundred peacewalkers begin the journey from Auschwitz to Hiroshima, filled with the Spirit of Peace from their time together.

Beyond Revenge and Despair

When we experience the kinds of violations that make us wonder if forgiveness and healing are possible, we often fall into the extremes of sorrow and anger, namely despair and vengeful rage. In the first, we are immobilized by our pain, unable to imagine a time or a way of being where the pain is not our primary state. In the latter, we react to the pain by striking back at the one who caused it. While both may feel like natural responses to terrible circumstances, we do have other choices.

Earlier in this chapter, I gave a definition of forgiveness as giving over or giving away that which impedes the free flow of love. To whom or to what are we giving over, or surrendering, our pain? We all have familiarity with beings or forces larger than ourselves on whom we call for assistance, in whom we take refuge, or on whose strength we rely. Depending on our belief systems, it may be the power of community; saints and angels; the natural forces of wind and water, earth and fire; religious figures or deities; our higher self; or God as we know and experience it, in different forms and by different names.

By releasing what hardens our heart to these forces that exist within and around us, that are more spacious expressions of who we really are, we are simply allowing the energy that has been tightened within us to return to its more expansive and natural state. When we can do this, despair and vengeful rage can change into something else.

Patricia Deer, a mediator and massage therapist from Chicago, Illinois, had such an experience with despair.

It is twenty-five years ago and my infant is crying. Her father grabs her from my arms, believing that I am the cause of her sobs. He throws me out of the house. Fortunately, our other children, three and two years old, are sound asleep, but they have seen many scenes like this. I walk in a park near our apartment. I am in the dark, inwardly and outwardly and I cry out for help. "What can I do with him?"

The answer came quickly, but not about him. It was about me. I saw my whole life, all my acts of generosity and kindness, as my own need to parade myself and look good. My life was ego-driven. Suddenly, surprisingly, I was filled with a sense of sweet clarity and sat down on the grass muttering over and over a phrase somehow remembered from a few Sunday School years of the past. "He restoreth my soul.'"

Opening the Heart of Peace

The richness of that moment took all anger and remorse from my consciousness. Ego was unmasked and replaced with something larger than myself. It was so large that it even affected my husband. I walked peacefully back home and to my astonishment, he peacefully returned the baby to my arms. At least for that evening, we found ease and contentment.

However, we lacked the tools to sustain that peace. A year later our fourth child was born; she died seven hours after birth because her lungs were underdeveloped. The death of the child prompted her father's one and only apology for his actions. He said the strain he had caused me had kept the child from developing normally. We had lived together for seven years, all of them emotionally abusive. After that rare apology, the abuse continued. I hung on by threads that grew thinner and thinner, as I tried to preserve my family.

When I finally left with the three children, ages five, four, and three, I was afraid and hiding. He used a private detective to find me and took the children. I was in agony; it took me four months in the courts before I could get the children back.

It was a bitter time. Lying in bed one night, my resentment raged at him for the ruin of all of our lives. I knew that resentment and bitterness were a difficult way to go through life, but I did not know how to be free of them. I was in despair.

Then the unexpected happened. I felt a strong presence pulling long thick bands of hatred from me. There seemed to be hands of love, ever so carefully drawing out of me years of venom that had congealed in cords. I lay there motionless, surrendering to this unusual sensation. The sinews of rancor that seemed to be twisted around every fiber of my being were gently unwound and drawn from me. I was left in a state of euphoria: light and well and free.

I spent the next twenty years raising my children alone, allowing them extensive visitation with their father. The peace I was given that night enabled me to move from a life of bitterness and fear to one of creativity and joy.

I call this phenomenon the forgiveness that comes through grace. Patricia opened herself to healing help from her higher power during her cold and bitter night walk. Having made herself available to the wisdom that inherently resides in her essential wholeness, that wisdom was able to express itself as grace, a state of apparently spontaneous healing.

Mammo Wudneh, an historian and journalist originally from Ethiopia, had a similar experience. Here is his story, as originally told by Michael Henderson on KBOO Radio in Portland, Oregon.

During World War II Mammo's parents and relatives were killed when the Italian Fascist Air Force bombed his village in Ethiopia. Thirty years later, by chance, he met an old man who, not realizing the connection, proudly told him that he was a pilot at the time of the Italian occupation of Ethiopia, and that he, together with the son of Mussolini, had bombarded this particular village.

Mammo shivered and became furious. He went to his room to get a pistol so he could take his revenge. "Yet, my conscience forced me to think twice," he says. "I begged God to show me the right direction and help to guide me. The answer came: If I killed the Italian Fascist, would my parents and relatives be alive? At a time when people all over the world forgive the past wrongdoing and live in peace and tolerance, if I killed an old man, does this not mean repeating the same mistake committed by Mussolini?"

Mammo thought it over. The next day he went back to the bar where he had met the pilot and told him his story. "He was shocked, he was trembling, thinking I was going to take revenge on him. I told him that I forgive him."

"I am sorry, sorry; please forgive me," the pilot replied, and they embraced.

"I also kissed him," says Mammo.

Forgiving Ourselves

A discussion of forgiveness would not be complete without a consideration of the need for self-forgiveness. While we may assign blame to those who have hurt us, we also assign guilt and shame to ourselves, both when we realize we have hurt others, and sometimes even when we ourselves have been injured, since many of us carry the belief that we must have done something to deserve being hurt.

As a child, I had two girls my age as close neighbors. At first it was just Judy and me, living next door to each other amid a combined handful of four brothers. We made up for all those boys by being sisters, in and out of each other's homes and lives daily. Then Bonnie moved across the street, and preadolescence hit at the same time. Bonnie was different—a different religion, different kind of family life—and I found myself drawn into her world. Judy was left behind.

This went on for about two years, even though I knew how hurt

Judy was, and even though my parents spoke to me about including her. In my pubescent selfishness, I didn't. Predictably, Bonnie floated out of my life shortly thereafter, while Judy has remained a true sister, a close and fast friend for fifty years. Though I apologized repeatedly to her for the hurt I know I caused her during that time, and though she has accepted my apology and managed her own healing process around this wound fairly easily, it took me much longer to forgive myself.

I have a personal forgiveness ritual that I used for this and similar situations, a ritual that has been influenced by two wise Native American women who are important in my life. I find a spot in the natural world where I can be alone. Sometimes I go to the edge of a river to scoop water over my shoulders, or I sit under a small waterfall and let the water wash over the top of my head; other times I lie down with my belly on the earth, or sit on a rock on a windy day. I offer to the elements whatever blame or shame I am carrying about myself, or about others. Then I let it all go, trusting the elements to wash away the hurts and flaws, rinsing me clean and fresh to start again. At first I wondered if I was polluting the environment by casting my "stuff" into the air or water or soil, but I soon realized that these are strong trans-formative forces, willing and able to help purify human pollution, so I give thanks for their help.

This is a great practice to do periodically, and works well for the big pieces of forgiveness I've needed to do in my life. However, I have also found that I can do this in miniature every day. Before I go to bed, I simply review my day, and if there were moments, as there invariably were, when I may have not loved as fully as I could, I offer that into the flame of a candle, to be transformed in the light.

Opening the Heart of Peace

The Apology Spectrum

"We don't say 'sorry' in this culture. It simply isn't done." Having said that, a peacebuilder I once worked with in a violent ethnic conflict took a deep breath and proceeded to apologize for the violence her people had unleashed against the other group. There was stunned silence, then much weeping in the room, as people felt the enormity of her surrender and the opening it created for making a new start in the relationship.

We have looked at one piece of the reconciliation puzzle, the forgiveness process, in which we change our own hearts to surrender the resentment we carry against ourselves and others. Now we turn our attention to another piece, the apology process, by which we right the wrongs we have perpetrated against others and find ways, through our words and actions, to say "Sorry" and to make amends.

My thinking on this subject is much affected by a story I heard many years ago through a video produced by Moral Rearmament called *Hope for Tomorrow* about a French women, Irene Laure. During the Second World War, Irene was active in the French Resistance, daily risking her life and the lives of her family to fight the injustice and hardship of the Nazi occupation. After the war, she was invited to an international meeting at the Moral Rearmament conference center in Caux, Switzerland, to consider the rebuilding of Europe. Hundreds of people attended. When a delegation from Germany walked in, Irene walked out. There was no way she was going to sit together with "them," the "enemy."

However, Irene didn't leave the conference, but instead went through three days of deep soul searching, after which she was able to meet a German woman face to face. In that meeting, she poured out her bitterness, but also heard from the German woman about her own pain and suffering during the war, and an apology for the fact that the Germans hadn't done enough to stop Hitler.

Later, Irene took the podium at the conference. While it would have made a good story had she, at that point, offered forgiveness to the Germans, she went one better and asked their forgiveness for the resentment and bitterness she had carried toward them. This surprise acknowledgment allowed a huge outpouring of feeling at the conference, and set the stage for a vast healing process between French and German citizens and, ultimately, governments, that evolved over the next several years.

What always touches me so much about this story is the fact that Irene was clearly not the aggressor in this case, and could easily have carried the victim torch with some public justification. Instead, she realized how she herself contributed to the broken hoop, and offered her apology for that. She demanded nothing from the Germans present; there was no quid pro quo, though I believe that, in fact, her comments did create a safe space in which the Germans were able to voice their regrets as well.

The other part of this story that is so instructive to me is that Irene followed up her words with actions. She went to Germany many times, and to other places around the world too, to repeat her apology and to do whatever she could to build new bridges of trust and understanding.

Irene's story illustrates all the elements of the apology spectrum: acknowledgment of her own responsibility, contrition or remorse, expression of regret, and restorative action.

Owning Up

One of our great American myths concerns George Washington and the cherry tree. In acknowledging his misdeed, Washington set before us a paradigm of honesty and responsibility that we, as individuals and as a nation, are still struggling to emulate.

In my journey as a human being and as a peacebuilder I have ample internal evidence of our great capacity for dodging responsibility for our actions. I myself am highly skilled at finding excuses for my behavior, in order to protect myself from facing the consequences. Because I seek to please others and avoid conflict, I am likely to backpedal furiously if I have said or done something that might anger another person or produce conflict.

I have a more-than-ample toolbox for this purpose. I deny, by suggesting I never really did or said what was reported. I project, by suggesting it must be someone else's problem. I evade, by deftly changing the subject. I procrastinate, by putting off an activity that might create tension. I defend, by finding a justification for my actions. I displace, by shifting the blame to another. I have so many skills in this area, I could get an advanced degree!

By the time I was twelve years old, I was already a wonderkid at not taking responsibility. During my two months at summer camp that year, I studied Junior Life Saving. On the day of the water test, I swam out to deep water with my instructor and went through all the proper holds and saves that would qualify me for this certificate. I did very well, and we began to swim back to shore. I was immensely proud of myself.

All of a sudden, my self-satisfied thoughts were interrupted by chaos. My instructor grabbed me around the head, and started thrashing around in the water, pushing me under in the process. I struggled to the surface to gasp some air, and she pushed me right back down again. Each time I came up, I would shout, "But that's not fair! That's not fair! The test was over!" She never said a word; she just kept pushing me under.

Finally, I realized I could keep protesting the injustice of the situation, or I could save her, and myself, from drowning. I chose the latter, and executed one of the more complex saving techniques I had been taught. Again, I was proud of myself for demonstrating such skill. That pride was short-lived, however. Because of my self-righteous attempts to make my unpreparedness somehow her fault, I failed the test.

Maybe because I am so aware of the difficulty I have with taking responsibility that I see it all around me. Our prisons are full of people who refuse to acknowledge what they have done, and our courts jammed with people who sue others either as a way of deflecting their own responsibility, or of demanding that the other own up to the harm they have caused, or both. Rarely do we hear, simply, "Yes, I did this. I'm sorry."

In the international arena, this reluctance to acknowledge the fruits of our actions can be extremely dangerous. Many large-scale international conflicts could have been eased or prevented in earlier stages had political leaders simply had the courage to acknowledge the responsibility of their side in hurting others. Instead, there is massive finger-pointing, and demands of what the other must do to correct things, with little or no attention paid to what our own side has contributed to the fray.

When people are hurt, they want recognition of that pain, and acknowledgment of the action that caused it. This is a precursor for an actual apology, and in some cases, is quite sufficient in itself for the reconciliation. When the acknowledgment is denied, they feel doubly violated; the bitterness deepens and the conflict escalates. The withholding of the acknowledgment can be a major obstacle to progress in the journey toward peace.

My colleague, John McDonald, tells of such a case.

The year was 1994, at the midpoint of the brutal civil war in Liberia. I was part of a team of facilitators working with leading figures from all the warring parties in the conflict. We took nine Liberians, men and women, Muslims and Christians, who represented the major tribes and factions in the war, to a safe haven in another country for a weeklong exploration of the possibilities for peacebuilding in Liberia.

We spent most of the first two days getting to know each other, encouraging the Liberians to talk about the history of their country, how the civil war had started, its impact on each one of them as individuals, and on their families. Each participant told amazing and often frightening stories. It became clear that each group lived in fear of the other. It also become clear that each blamed the conflict on the United States government and its people, for acts of commission and omission throughout the 150-year existence of Liberia. There was little acknowledgment of their own group's responsibility for the current conflict.

The discussion finally reached the point where I felt I had to say something that would help bring the group into the present, so that we could, together, look to the future. I said that I had listened carefully, and had heard all of their stories and their views of the history of their country and their conflict, and that I was deeply moved by their hurt, their sorrow, and their pain.

Everyone knew that I was a retired ambassador, with a forty-year career in the U.S. State Department. Although I was not present at this event in any official capacity, still my former association with the U.S. government gave me a certain stature. I said that, speaking unofficially on behalf of the American people and of the American government, I humbly apologized to them for our transgressions against Liberia, and asked their forgiveness for the things we had done and not done over the past 150 years that contributed to the current situation.

This was a powerful moment. There was a stunned silence in the room that lasted for a long time. Then the group went on to discuss critical issues and options for peacebuilding. Although the apology was never mentioned or discussed during the rest of the week, I was told later that it was the turning point in the program, and was instrumental in bringing us all together so that we could begin to envision a peaceful future for Liberia.

I remember a newspaper article some years ago that touched me deeply. It described an acknowledgment ritual in a particular region of Albania, where multigenerational blood feuds between extended families were a way of life. The families stood facing each other on the hillsides, and the facilitator (I vaguely remember it was a priest) invited the head of first one family then the other to step forward and acknowledge that their family had killed this person and that person from the other family, enumerating the deaths by name. They then expressed regret and a desire to stop the cycle of killing. Following these acknowledgments, there was much embracing and celebration.

One thing that stood out for me in this story, besides the power of the reconciliation, was the double-sided nature of what was being acknowledged. While there are certainly cases of single-sided aggression and oppression, most deep conflicts are interactive situations in which rarely is only one side totally at fault while the other is pure and clean of all transgression. The usual pattern is for an initial hurt to be returned, and thus a cycle of attack and counterattack, or blame and revenge, ensues. If this goes on long enough, it becomes nearly impossible to sort out who started what. All parties have some piece of the responsibility; all have contributed in some way, and need to acknowledge their parts, without excusing or justifying because of what the other did.

Why this should be so extremely hard for us to do is a great mystery to me. Of course, some obvious "reasons" come to mind: we don't want to feel guilty; we don't want to be punished or reprimanded; we don't want to feel ashamed or humiliated; we don't want to be the first to acknowledge our role in the conflict lest we lose political power or personal "face"; we don't want to be held legally or financially responsible for cleaning up the mess.

Undoubtedly there are other stories we tell ourselves about why it is better not to own up to what we have done, but these are all superficial and ultimately selfish excuses. It strikes me as sad that we are willing to allow great harm and suffering to continue and wounds to fester rather than to face the consequences of our behavior. In fact, the longer we let things go, the worse they become. Our hurts do not necessarily disappear with time; rather, they tend to become embedded in the fabric of our relationships.

Fifty-plus years after World War II, we in America are still talking about the political viability of official apologies and reasonable restitution for interning Japanese citizens, and more than a hundred years after the Civil War, we are still discussing the pros and cons of an apology for slavery. Only in the last few years, after decades of abuse, has Canada apologized to its First Nations people for government policies that forcibly took Native children from their parents and pushed them into foster homes and boarding schools, where their culture, their religion, their families and, in many cases, their safety and well-being were denied them. The U.S. government, and many of the churches involved, have yet to acknowledge their role in similar actions in this country. While the authorities consider the political implications of acknowledging and apologizing for these events, the victims continue to suffer.

One theory I have about why it is so difficult to hold ourselves accountable for our actions, and for the harm caused by them, is that we confuse blame with responsibility. We think that if we own up to having done wrong deeds, our "badness" will show. In other words, we hold ourselves (and each other) blameworthy—literally, worthy of blame or shame. We confuse the being and the doing; assigning ourselves and others negative labels and ascribing negative qualities for our actions that produce negative results. Blaming is a judgmental activity that tends to impede the process of reconciliation, because the one blamed will either wallow in shame or defend against the blame.

Taking responsibility, on the other hand, is an empowering activity that acknowledges a simple truth: Our actions inevitably affect others, and set in motion certain results. Taking responsibility, or holding others accountable for their behavior, focuses on the "doing" aspect of our humanness rather than on the "being" aspect. If we have done something that wounds the sacred hoop, we can correct our action, make amends, and make different choices in the future. In that way, responsibility reminds us of the potency of our will, our power to both respond to situations through conscious choice, and to shape our lives proactively.

The issue of taking responsibility reminds me of the river of love. The endless stream of love exists, whether we choose to immerse ourselves in it or not. So too with responsibility. Our thoughts, words, and actions do set in motion certain consequences, for others and for ourselves, whether we choose to recognize this or not. We are more powerful and effective in our lives if we work with what is, rather than against it.

This whole discussion leads me right back to where I ended the inquiry about forgiveness. If in fact we are reasonably conversant with the tools of self-forgiveness and purification, we can face into the consequences of our actions and own up to our responsibilities. If we can recall that love is our natural state, and however we may have separated ourselves from that or denied that in another can be corrected, then we can right the wrongs we have enacted.

Righting the Wrongs

To further reconciliation, we may need to do more than acknowledge our responsibility and say, "Sorry." We may need take action that restores a sense of justice or makes amends for our wrongdoing. Once we have set a course of events in motion, an apology does not necessarily stop the unfolding of all the consequences.

For the U.S. government, for instance, to apologize to African Americans for slavery would be a big step, but it would not, by itself, reverse the years of oppression and injustice, nor erase the institutionalized racism that still exists in our housing, educational, economic, and other systems. The damage already done cannot be undone, though further damage can be prevented and the past, at the very least, acknowledged.

I had my own early experience with restorative justice. In a wild fling of adolescent rebellion, I joined a friend in what we considered to be a grand practical joke. It was the last days of summer camp, and we decided to leave a little good-bye "message." We went around late one night with a pin, poking holes in everyone's toothpaste tubes, so that when the girls went to brush their teeth in the morning, toothpaste would ooze out everywhere. In our fourteen-year-old minds, we thought this was hysterically funny.

Our camp director thought otherwise. She called it vandalism. We were required to go around to every single person in camp, gather information on the type and size of their toothpaste, then pay for replacing it.

At the time, I naturally thought the response was way too harsh, but of course I was busy honing my skills of evading responsibility in those days. In retrospect, I can see the beauty of the response. We were simply asked to own up to the consequences of our actions (people no longer had usable toothpaste, even if it was the last day of camp), and to fix the situation we had created. I wish all matters of righting wrongs were so simple.

The notion of restorative justice is spreading in our courts and legal system. The idea that there is more to justice than punishment for a

Opening the Heart of Peace

crime or exacting retribution through the courts is capturing the imagination of judges and lawyers. The practice of assigning community service for certain types of crimes is an attempt to move in that direction. So too is the growing practice of mediation, which seeks to help each party to a dispute understand the needs and interests of the other party, so that they can come to a joint resolution that benefits all. Sometimes the restorative action occurs simply by being present to one another's pain.

Andrea Bassin, from Albuquerque, New Mexico, tells a story of a mediation she facilitated where the initial drive of the parties was for restitution and revenge, but where the process of mediation uncovered many layers of feeling and intention that actually led to a very different outcome.

The case involved a man, Juan, whose car had been damaged at the local high school by a teenaged Hispanic female whom I'll call Ana, in an act of anger that left $1,400 worth of destruction. A mediation was arranged to discuss possible restitution.

I met with each of the parties separately in a pre-mediation session. The meeting with Ana consisted of her telling me that she did damage the car, but that she had done it out of anger at Juan's daughter Rosa. Rosa had made a snide comment about how Ana's appearance was the reason that her father had become afflicted with cancer. In reaction to this comment, and with some peer pressure from her friends, Ana retaliated by slashing one of the tires, keying the hood of the car, and kicking and denting two of the doors.

After discovering the damage to the car, Rosa had immediately apologized for what she had said, knowing that her comments had been the reason for the destruction of her car. She had said this hurtful comment because Ana had begun to date her ex-boyfriend, with whom Rosa was still in love.

Ana came to the mediation with the belief that the incident had been resolved, because she and Rosa had discussed the situation. Ana had offered all of her saved allowance to the daughter ($400), but Rosa had refused to take it. Because she thought the problem had been resolved, Ana was very surprised and scared to be called into the juvenile court for a mandatory mediation.

On the other side of the dispute was Juan. He was furious at Ana for destroying his car, and was fearful that she was mean enough to harm his daughter. He had ignored Rosa's explanation that she had said something offensive to Ana. He also ignored Rosa's offer to pay for the damage to the car. Basically, he thought that Ana had intimidated Rosa into taking the rap.

He was also angry with the courts for not doing more to punish Ana and force her to pay the full restitution. At one point, while telling the story, he turned to me and told me that I had to force Ana to pay for the damages, and I also had to send her to jail. He said this in a threatening and forceful tone. After I explained the mediation process to him again for the second time, he questioned why his own son, who had damaged a car with spray paint, was not allowed to go to mediation for having committed the same offense.

Next, I brought the two parties together and suggested that they tell each other what happened to bring them here to the table. After each person told their side of the story, Ana apologized, on her own account, for the damage she had done. She offered the $400 again, and showed empathy toward Juan for having his son in the detention center. Ana acknowledged that she had been let off easy, but was thankful that she did not end up in jail because it might have caused her father's illness to get worse.

Juan accepted Ana's apology, and apologized for his daughter's comments. At this time, he not only refused Ana's $400, he also offered his own money to her father for medical expenses. The session ended with the two parties hugging each other and both crying.

What has been restored here in this story is not the money to repair a car, but a sense of caring; of belonging to each other. The sacred hoop has moved one small step toward being mended. But what of those situations where the damage done is far greater than $1,400, far beyond any price in dollar terms?

What can we possibly do the right the wrongs that flowed, and continue to flow, from the conquest and genocide of the native peoples of the Americas, or the kidnapping and enslavement of Africans for the slave trade? What actions would be enough; what would restore the broken trust; what would truly heal the wounds?

I ask these questions because I work and travel in places around the world that are dealing with today's legacies of yesterday's oppression: centuries of colonialism, imperialism, sexism, and racism. We like to think that, those days being in the past, we no longer need to worry about such excesses. We forget the myriad and subtle ways that past conquests continue to influence present realities, not just for individual people—descendants of slavery or colonialism—but for whole systems and societies.

One of my favorite stories is of a poignant moment in Costa Rica, when the sacred hoop was mended, if only briefly, in the 500-plus–year-old relationship between the indigenous peoples of the Americas and the Europeans who came, conquered, and settled here. My spiritual teacher, the Venerable Dhyani Ywahoo, from Lincoln, Vermont, was one of the principals in this story.

In 1989 I was invited to participate in an international conference in Costa Rica called "Seeking the True Meaning of Peace," along with several other prominent spiritual and religious leaders, including His Holiness the Dalai Lama and the Papal Legate to Costa Rica. I wondered why I, a Native American woman from North America, was asked to represent the indigenous people when there were surely local traditional leaders right there in Costa Rica.

When I arrived, I looked carefully around the streets, and noticed many Native people. I asked around until I found a Native group that had an office in the city. There I asked if I might speak with the medicine people of the region. They arranged an arduous trip of several days, through the jungle beyond all roads and across swollen rivers by canoe, into the mountains of the rain forest. There I met the Awas, or spiritual leaders of the Bri Bri people, the people indigenous to that land who still maintained their traditional spiritual ways.

I told the Awas of the conference to be held in San José, and especially of a prayer service that would take place in the Basilica in Cartega, outside the capital city. I had been invited to offer prayers there, along with the other spiritual leaders, and, though I knew there was political and religious opposition to this, I extended an invitation to one of the Awas to join me on the podium. He agreed, and we began the long trip back to the city, arriving just in time for the procession into the Cathedral.

The Basilica was packed, inside and out, with Costa Ricans eager to participate in such a special event. Many citizens of Costa Rica are of mixed blood, with an indigenous heritage, yet have denied this background and felt great shame about their origins. When the Awa and I arrived, a stunned hush came over the crowd. People realized instinctively the power of the moment. For an indigenous leader to stand at the center of the mightiest symbol of Catholic power in the land and make prayers, in the company of exalted internationally acclaimed spiritual leaders from other traditions, was an enormously transformative moment. As we walked down the aisle together, it felt to me like a great light had entered the church, illuminating us and making clear the shifting of emotions and the importance of the event.

The Awa spoke simply, offering prayers and telling of the history of his people. One Bri Bri leader had been drawn and quartered in that very place for refusing to be enslaved centuries before. The Basilica itself was founded on a spot where an indigenous woman discovered a natural stone picture of the Madonna and Child. As he spoke, a doorway opened to a past without rancor and to a future where the voices of the indigenous could be heard again. Once more, a people could take pride in their traditions and sacred heritage, and the indigenous people could claim again their rightful place in the sacred circle of prayer and spirit in Costa Rica, alongside and inside the very Church that had conquered and oppressed them 500 years before.

When the Awa completed his prayers, there was a pregnant

pause, in which one could feel the power of forgiveness and recognition fill the silence. Then, from inside the Basilica and from outside in the packed plaza came the roar of applause. Those present knew intuitively that in that moment the original people had been restored to their rightful place in the sacred hoop, and could again and forevermore walk with dignity and pride in their own land.

Stories like this are heartening to me, because they remind me that even the biggest, toughest breaks in the circle of life can be blessed with healing by the Spirit of Peace. Another example that inspires me comes from Richmond, Virginia. There, in 1993, private citizens in the "Hope in the Cities" project, in cooperation with leaders of metropolitan Richmond, convened the first national conference called "Healing the Heart of America: An Honest Conversation on Race, Reconciliation, and Responsibility."

The choice of Richmond was not accidental. As the heart and capital of the southern Confederacy, Richmond was a major port for the slave trade. The program included a day-long unity walk through history, where people of all races gathered, several hundred strong, and with prayers and songs, stories and candles, flowers and tears, walked a circuit of places in the Richmond landscape that had special historical meaning to Native, white, and black Americans, educating one another about what really happened there so long ago.

They visited a Native American burial ground; a Confederate Soldier memorial; the first Jewish cemetery in the city; Manchester Docks, one of the largest ports of entry in the nation for kidnapped Africans; Lumpkins Jail, the auction block and holding cells for Africans being sold into slavery, which later became the site of Virginia

Union University, the state's first African American college; and St. John's Church, where Patrick Henry gave his famous speech, "Give me liberty or give me death."

This powerful event demonstrated vividly that history can be used as a healing tool. Did this event heal the history of racism in Richmond? No. Did it impose full justice for the wrongs done to African Americans through the institution of slavery? No. Did it improve the schools in black neighborhoods? No. Did it open the door to better job opportunities for black women? Probably not.

What it did do was restore the dignity, the right of other-than-white Americans to take their full place in the circle and be heard and seen in all their pain and glory. Is that enough? No. Is it a place to start? Certainly. In fact, this program spurred similar action in dozens of other cities in the United States and around the world, leading to a whole series of dialogues, special forums, and other events continuing the theme of "an honest conversation on race, reconciliation, and responsibility."

As peacebuilders in our homes and communities, we may not be able to deliver pure justice and restore all that has been lost when we have wronged one another. But we can commit to the journey and take the first step. In that first step, if we open our hearts, the river of love will carry us along, to the next step, and the next.

Letting the Heart Shatter a Thousand Times

I said earlier that the third aspect of reconciliation, after forgiveness and righting of wrongs, is to encompass and embrace the suffering of others. By doing so, we meet one another at the core of our shared humanity, heart to heart, developing empathy and compassion.

In my work, I have experienced situations of great human suffering. As a therapist, I've engaged with individuals and families living with anguish from physical and sexual abuse; from loss, death, and disease; and from the many ways we have learned to hurt the ones we love the most.

It is, however, as an international peacebuilder that I have confronted the greatest suffering. I have been to the hellholes of the world, where torture, genocide, terrorism, brutality, rank injustice, and senseless violence are the daily fare and intergenerational heritage of millions of people.

I have been to these places, and met the people who live in such zones of agony. It is quite one thing to read about the finding of mass graves in Rwanda, or the rape camps in Bosnia. It is quite another to meet a survivor of one of those camps, who says that, had she known what it would be like beforehand, she would have found a way—any way—to kill herself first. People often ask me how I can stand it, meeting this level of evil and of suffering.

When I first started, my natural reaction was to close off against the depths of pain; to bring down a wall between me and its victims, in the fantasy that I could protect myself from their suffering and thus remain effective and "professional." I soon learned the folly of this approach. Pushing against the pain, or distancing myself from it, only left it hanging around, unaddressed yet persistent in its subtle effect on my whole being.

I learned, instead, to open to the pain, and let my heart break, again and again if necessary, until it lies shattered in a million pieces. Each

Opening the Heart of Peace

time I do this, my heart becomes bigger and more spacious. The more I let myself accept the pain, the more love and compassion can move through me. When I tighten up, the love flow is decreased. When I keep all channels open, without attachment or repulsion, the love rushes through.

This lesson was reinforced for me in a graphic way one evening during a concert. I attended the event, expecting a certain kind of gentle, melodic music. Instead, the music was harsh and blaring. It was so loud, in fact, that I felt physically and psychically assaulted by the sound. I thought about leaving, but realized to do so would have meant stepping over about a dozen people, many of whom were elderly, sitting between me and the aisle. I chose instead to practice this discipline of staying open to the pain. I let the sound move through me, offering no resistance in body or mind against which it could push or to which it could adhere. I simply accepted the sound as it was, without reaction, until an intermission came and I could politely leave.

My friend, on the other hand, had the same experience I did of the distressing nature of the music, but he tightened himself up against it, reacting in a protective mode by gritting his teeth, scrunching his shoulders, and otherwise trying not to let it get to him. Later that evening, he was in great physical pain from all the tightness; I was fine.

The Compassionate Presence

Accepting the pain of others is not the same as taking it on our own shoulders or letting it harm us. Accepting the pain of others is remembering that in our web of interconnectedness, one service I can provide is to return love for suffering. By allowing the suffering to wash through me, acknowledging it, feeling it, but not energizing it, my heart remains open and free, a gateway for compassion, which, in Buddhist terms, is the desire to relieve the suffering of others.

While loving compassion may not by itself cure the ills and right the wrongs of the world, it will certainly be a significant factor in our healing. I think of a small child who skins her knee and runs to Mommy for comfort. Mommy's kiss and hug are as much the healing medicine as the iodine and Band-Aid.

Because love is our natural spiritual state, the inherent expression of our divine nature, it has the power to transform or lift a situation into a higher frequency. By sounding the note or vibrating the power of love into a situation of pain, we are actually freeing the unexpressed love that is bound up in that situation. The love that comes through us acts like a magnet, attracting that freed energy as surely as a moth is attracted to the light. In this way, the very molecules of our being are realigned to the original template of our wholeness, and pain recedes.

I learned firsthand about the power of this type of realignment when I was least expecting it. I had the opportunity to meet with His Holiness the Dalai Lama about some business matters. Having seen him before in many conferences and small gatherings, and having met many other great spiritual teachers in other settings, I approached the meeting quite matter of factly. Though of course I felt honored to have a private meeting with him, I was not feeling any great awe or reverence. I was certainly not expecting any mystical moments.

My casual attitude made what happened all the more astonishing. As he drew the meeting to a close, His Holiness held my hand between both of his and walked me out the door and down the hall. My physical body had a profoundly unexpected reaction. I suddenly felt as if every cell in my body was being reorganized to harmonize with his energy field, which is considered by Tibetan Buddhists to be a radiation of the pure energy of compassion. I was deeply struck by the intensity of what happened. He was vibrating at a high frequency of love, even though we were talking about mundane matters, and his touch allowed me to vibrate in phase with him.

This simple principle, by which sounding the note of love changes the vibration of a situation, is at play all the time, though we may not be aware of it. An anonymous peacebuilder from Washington, D.C., tells of a family experience where her unexpected compassion changed an entrenched family dynamic.

In early August, I drove with my parents to Minneapolis. We were dining in a Vietnamese restaurant when the three of us all observed a man and a woman walking past the restaurant, connected to each other by a rope that was tied around their waists. My mother pointed to them, chuckling, so I smiled too, and told my parents of a well-documented art project from the 1970s in which two performance artists were tied together by an eight-foot rope for a year, requiring them to live collaboratively.

My mother responded, raising her voice to state her opinion of the artistic merit of this performance project. She found its content not worthy of placement in the category of "art." She went on to say, "It's no wonder the National Endowment for the Arts is being progressively defunded, if this is the type of work that contemporary artists are proposing when requesting federal funding."

My mother and I have a history of locking horns, particularly during debates over issues such as "What constitutes art?" Typically, I would have followed her lead, raised my voice to match, and argued passionately, and the debate would likely have escalated rapidly into an argument. This time, something very different happened. I was, quite literally, overwhelmed by a sense of compassion for my mother.

I can best describe this as a visceral reaction, in which I viewed the words that formed my mother's opinion as having palpability. My internal response was a desire to lift the weight of what I perceived as judgment off her shoulders. My external response was to lower my voice and tell her that I understood her response to be based on her view of certain kinds of artmaking principles, which I know are important to her, and that others do feel this work to have merit within our contemporary culture. The debate did not escalate; instead, it died down and ended, allowing for other conversations to begin, with no visible hard feelings.

The next morning my father took me aside to tell me how pleased he was at the way in which I responded the previous night. Because of our history, he had expected me to engage in a full-fledged argument with my mother. This time the pattern had been broken.

To reach a state of compassion, we may need first to experience empathy. This is the ability "to put ourselves in the shoes of another," to see and know and feel how things are for them. When we are in conflict, we are usually thinking about our own suffering, not the other person's. By locking ourselves away from each other in this way, we ensure that no one gets heard or acknowledged, and reconciliation becomes nearly impossible. Somehow, we need to find the bridge that will allow us to keep the integrity of our own experience, while touching that of the other at the same time.

Molly De Maret, from Dixon, New Mexico, tells of a mediation she facilitated in which this bridge was created.

> Last summer I was the mediator for two girls (Ann, twelve, and Julie, thirteen) who had been in a fight after school. Julie had jumped Ann "for no apparent reason" just before the end of the school year. Ann's mother reported the incident to the police, and the case was referred to the Juvenile Victim-Offender Mediation Program.
>
> In the pre-mediation with Ann, I learned that Ann was terrified because she had received several anonymous death threats (which she attributed to Julie), warning her not to attend the middle school in the fall. Ann and her mother took these threats seriously, and Ann was considering going to school in another town. Though she was afraid to meet with Julie, she hoped to learn why Julie disliked her so much, since they hardly knew each other.
>
> From Julie I learned that the fight was mostly due to peer pressure, rather than from any real dislike for Ann. She said that she was not responsible for the threats, but had a good idea who might be, and that she didn't think they were serious. She had no personal issues to resolve with Ann. She just wanted to get the mediation over with so she wouldn't be in trouble anymore.
>
> During the mediation, Julie seemed to understand how frightened Ann really was about the coming school year. She took Ann under her wing, reassuring her that she was not in any real danger,

and agreeing to tell the other girls to leave her alone. She also said she thought they were only picking on Ann because she was so pretty. Ann went from being a terrified little girl to one with hope for the coming school year and a potential new friend, and Julie went from being indifferent to Ann to caring about her and wanting to help her. As the mediation ended, shy smiles and phone numbers were exchanged.

Eileen Borris, who runs a peacebuilding organization in Paradise Valley, Arizona, gives us another example of the power of empathy and compassion to feed reconciliation. She tells of a situation involving Palestinian women living during the Intifada, under military occupation by the Israelis. On the day of the event she witnessed, she writes,

Emotions were running high, one moment very excited and the next very depressed. I was going to a nearby town to give a workshop for the women there. As I was walking toward the building a shot flew past me. When I got inside, I found out that the electricity was turned off, probably on purpose. This was the reality the women dealt with every day because of the occupation.

The workshop began with the women telling stories of husbands being killed, sons thrown in jail, and children hurt and maimed. Fists were in my face, as the women yelled, "You are an American, why aren't you doing anything for us?"

In the midst of all this anger, a woman began telling a story. She said that one day her son ran out of the house. He was throwing stones at some soldiers and was caught. The mother went to the soldiers, demanding to have her son back. Suddenly she looked into their eyes and saw fear. She was astonished to think that these soldiers were as afraid as she was!

At that moment, something shifted inside of her. She felt compassion, and told the soldiers that she wanted her son to stay inside so he could not bring harm to himself or to others. She began to feel at peace with the soldiers, something she never experienced before. She went to the main army headquarters to request her son back, and to her amazement he was released to her. When the woman finished telling her story, another woman said, "Now I understand compassion."

Opening the Heart of Peace: Letting Go

If we are to understand and experience reconciliation, we need to go through a shift like the one this Palestinian woman describes. The shift is the moment the heart opens, and whatever we have been holding moves ever so slightly aside to make room for a new understanding.

This shift can be the result of hard work and conscious choice, or it can be a gift of grace; it can result from meeting the other person heart to heart, or from experiencing a piece of the sacred hoop restored to its rightful place. However it happens, the shift is the moment when we open a new door on a familiar scene, and nothing is ever the same afterward.

To be able to receive the new energy or information coming in, we need to make space for it. That means letting go of that which no longer serves us. Letting go is, I believe, one of the most important skills a human being can develop. It is what allows us to stay in the river of love, without putting the brakes on our journey by clinging to branches along the way. To let go is to release what we feel comfortable or secure hanging on to, and allow ourselves to flow with the natural impermanence of life into the next turn of the river, without necessarily knowing what we will find there. Some say, "Let go and let God." My variation on that theme is, "Let go and let love. . . ."

What is it we need to let go of for reconciliation? It may be the pain or the bitterness we are feeling. Perhaps it is the anger or desire for revenge—to punish or strike back. Maybe it is our attachment to the victim script, or to a particular story we have convinced ourselves is the only truth. It could be our need to be right, our desire to be on top, our need for control, or our sense of what justice would look like in a given situation. Perhaps it is fear of humiliation and shame, or a resistance to facing into our loss and completing our mourning, or simply our pride and ego.

Whatever it is we need to let go of, ultimately, it is some variation of fear. That's because, if we are not in a state of love, we are in a state of fear. As love is the glue of our inherent oneness, so fear is the primal anxiety that comes from mistakenly believing we are separate. Fear closes us off; love opens us up. When fear is released, love can flow in and through us. If love comes knocking, and our heart is so full of fear that we cannot open the door, a great opportunity is missed.

Often what makes letting go possible is our separating the lessons in the experience from the experience itself. I understand this as extracting the essence or meaning so I can release the form, or the package it came in. I remember the moment I first understood this notion. I was divorcing; I had cancer; I was a single mother—I was terrified of what my immediate future held. I had attended a weekend

Opening the Heart of Peace

residential workshop on some topic or other, and the community of learners had bonded deeply, as often happens in such settings. When Sunday afternoon came around, and the workshop was over, I didn't want to go back to my life's frightening circumstances. I wanted to hang on to the wonderful people, the warm experience, the sense of group safety.

One of the facilitators felt my clinging, and shared with me one of the major paradoxes of human experience. He said, "If you want to have it, you have to let it go." It took me many years to unfold the mystery of this paradox. I finally came to an understanding that I can retain the essence of an experience while letting go of its outer form or structure. To do this, I must reach into the very core of any experience and extract the essential lessons.

Extracting the lessons comes through asking the right questions: "What is this experience all about in my life? What can I learn from it? What opportunities is it affording me for taking my next steps on this wild and wondrous human-spiritual journey? How is this situation helping me grow in love, or in taking responsibility for what I create? How can it help me remember myself as truly divine, one with all that is? What new information or skill can I draw from this that I can use in other situations? What essential meaning can I integrate from this, so that I no longer feel the need to cling to the outer form?"

Drawing out the lessons is like emptying a box. I have a box that holds certain objects. Once I sort through the box, throwing away those objects I no longer want and finding a different way to keep those I do, I have no further need for that particular box. In the case of reconciliation, the box is the outward expression of the relationship. If

I change the inner meaning, taking what is useful from the box, I can find a new and more appropriate container for the relationship.

The ultimate challenge of letting go has to do with one of the great paradoxes of human life, which is that we are each whole and unbreakable, yet in need of mending what is broken in our lives. We need to actively release what precipitates the brokenness in order to recall the wholeness.

Here again, we need to think simultaneously of two levels of reality: the particular and the absolute; the drop of water and the ocean. In our everyday, matter-of-fact life, our hearts are chipped, scuffed, poked, bashed, and sometimes broken in our attempts to love and be loved. In our absolute, divine and holy nature, we are Love incarnate, one with the sacred circle of life, inviolate, whole, and wholly unbreakable. Our task is to come again and again to remember that wholeness, and the ultimate task of reconciliation is to reconcile ourselves with that remembrance. With time and practice, we might do this with ever greater speed, ease, and grace.

In my inner life, just as the Spirit of Peace inhabits the ideal world of my hopes and dreams for peace and harmony, so too is there another great being who carries the ideal of Love. I call this being the Angel of Love. I imagine the Angel of Love and the Spirit of Peace as partners, entwined in a single dance to set loose vast energies of love and peace on the planet, so that humanity might remember itself as it truly is, a single, sacred circle of life.

For me to receive this message, and concretely incorporate it into my everyday life, I need to be constantly letting go of whatever attitudes, feelings, beliefs, patterns, urges, or fears may hinder that ultimate reconciliation. Only then can I reach beyond my small self into the realm where the power of love and the joy of peace simply are.

When I can do that, I can draw down whatever I need to mend what simply appears to be broken. When I can do that, I can better care for all those precious beings who are my relatives, to whom I belong, and in whose keeping my heart is placed. When I can do that, I have touched the heart of the one, holy, heart, and the Spirit of Peace lives through me.

What a blessing.

Practice Letting Go

Here are two simple ways to experience the power of love for mending what seems to be broken, while strengthening the true unbreakability of the human heart and spirit.

1. Meditative Practice for Letting Go

Again, center home, aligning the spine and focusing on the cycle of your breath. Sink into and find that now-familiar place of deep inner peace. Think of a relationship in your life that calls for reconciliation. Focus your attention on your heart, and notice how it is constricted regarding this relationship. What feelings or thoughts are you holding on to?

Pick one of these that is impeding the flow of love in your heart, that you are ready and willing to change, and breathe into it. Allow the breath to soften what is hardened, gently easing the tightness. As you prepare to release this obstacle to love, first ask yourself how it has served you. You had this reaction for a reason that made sense at one time, even if it no longer serves you well. Be grateful for the lessons it has brought you, is bringing you even in this moment, and, when you are ready, release it on the out-breath into the vastness of space, to be recycled like compost into something more nourishing. Sit for a moment with this release. How do you feel? What, if anything, takes the place or fills the space left by that which you have put aside? Imagine the other party to this relationship in front of you. What would you want to say to them in this moment about what just happened?

2. Action Practice for Letting Go

Again, think of a relationship in your life that is ripe for reconciliation. Your task is to design and perform a simple ritual that will cleanse the negative energy of the relationship and revivify the stream of love between the two of you. Your first choice is whether to do this ritual by yourself, or whether to actually approach the other party and invite them to do it with you. Either way is fine.

As you design your ritual, think of other rituals that have touched you deeply. Try to identify the factors that were so powerful. Use that information as you create your ceremony. You might want to consider such elements as symbols that have important meaning, sounds or movements that can express the significance of the event, a way of cleansing or releasing what no longer serves, and a way of welcoming or celebrating a new quality in the relationship. You might also want to invoke some larger forces, such as the forces of nature or spiritual energies. There is no right or wrong in creating ritual. Whatever has meaning for you, whatever invites and enhances that shift in your heart, so that love can flow more freely, is appropriate in your ritual.

Go ahead and perform the ritual. How do you feel now? Sometimes, when we experience something really powerful, it is best not to diffuse that power by discussing it right away. Let the experience of the ritual wash through the many dimensions of your being, just being aware of any shifts or insights that may arise.

FOUR

Breathing peace,
I change the world.

Unleashing the Power of Peace

Moving to Action

CLAUDINE SCHNEIDER was a member of Congress during the Cold War period. Acting creatively, she was able transcend the "us versus them" paradigm of those days and build new bridges between traditional adversaries.

I had been in Congress for a few years, despite my lifelong distaste for politics. Then, one day, members were invited to a classified briefing about the latest activities in Central America. The emphasis was particularly on what the Soviets were doing there, and on our intended political and military response. I had seen and heard many such briefings, but this one disturbed me greatly. All night I tossed and turned.

The next day, I had lunch with my friend George Brown, Representative from California. I related to him how distressed I was about the briefing. I was concerned that the possible scenarios as I understood them could, I believed, lead to World War III. There must be something we could do.

Having been to the Soviet Union in 1973, and having met and interacted with so many wonderful people there, I kept thinking that if we could only get the decision makers from our respective lands together, or at least those aspiring to the top positions, we might get them around the same table and talk about our families, our joys and fears, and that would make a difference.

"Let's do something, George," I said.

"Use satellites," was his terse reply. (George Brown was my colleague on the Space, Science, and Technology Committee, and had always been intrigued with anything having to do with space.)

"What do you mean?" I said.

"Use the satellites to hook us and them up."

"Brilliant !" I said, and we set to work raising the money to do a pilot project.

We brought in someone to facilitate and someone to film the discussion, and convened a meeting with U.S. leaders and members of the Supreme Soviet, to have a conversation and design a six-part series that would address how each of us viewed our actions on a variety of issues (Central America, the environment). We shopped the concept around, and ABC responded positively. We negotiated to have it run live and unedited, which left us with the *Nightline* time slot, and arranged to have Peter Jennings as the moderator.

The series aired in the United States and repeatedly in the Soviet Union. ABC received an Emmy for it, which they soon turned over to us. But most important, many believe that because this series showed again and again in the Soviet Union, gradually the ideas of free speech and democracy permeated the country. Perhaps we contributed in some small way to *glasnost*.

Spiritual Lesson 4:
We Are Peacebuilders in Every Moment

If we think of peacebuilding as bringing right relationship into manifestation from the ideal to the tangible, then we need to understand the spiritual principles of manifestation, which have to do with how we shape the natural and neutral flow of energy.

Scientists in the twentieth century have discovered what mystics from all eras and cultures have known instinctively—that the basic "stuff" of life is energy; that what we know as matter is, as Einstein discovered, simply energy in motion. To work with form, to build, sculpt, and define our material world, therefore, we need to know how to work with energy.

Manifestation comes about in three stages. First is the contact with the ideal. We can understand that the first step in building a house would be to think about why we want this house. What value will it bring in our lives? What kind of home do we want? Is this merely a shelter for our physical bodies, or do we want a home where love can flourish, where people can live and grow together? Is our home also a work space? A play space? A prayer space? A place to practice our craft or art? A place for our children to grow?

When we address these questions, we are touching our dreams and hopes, our visions and our aspirations; in short, we are touching our highest ideals—the innate aspects of our divine nature. To bring these ideals into concrete form, however, we must do more than simply dream about them. We must engage our will.

Free will is a quality unique to human beings. We can, indeed we do, choose how we are and what we do in every moment. Sometimes our choices are so unconscious or routine that we don't even recognize them as choices—we comb our hair in the morning, and don't necessarily think about choosing to do so. Other choices are deeply patterned and conditioned by repetition and indoctrination. We may, for example, eat cereal for breakfast because that's what our mother gave us every morning of our childhood, or we may use polite forms of expression because our parents and teachers were rigorous in teaching us to do so.

When it comes to major life choices, we tend to be more conscious about possibilities and consequences. If we put insulation in the attic of our new home, it might cost more now but save in heating expenses over time. If, like the three little pigs, we build with straw or sticks instead of with bricks, we may not have a house at all after the first storm blows by. In such situations, the act of choosing requires that we align our will with our goal or purpose. If we want a house to stand for many years, we will use bricks. If we want a temporary, cool dwelling for one summer only, we might use straw.

So the first principle of manifestation is to engage the will and align it with our purpose. We even have a saying: "Where there is a will, there's a way." I have found that when that purpose relates to an ideal, there is great power and energy in the act of willing its realization. It's like the drop of water and the ocean. If my intention is for something to benefit myself alone, or some aspect of my lower nature, my will has the energy of a single drop. But if my intention is for something that bene- fits many, or that touches some aspect of my higher nature where I rec- ognize my connection to all that is, the will has the energy of the whole ocean. When my individual will is aligned with Divine Will, the inher- ent order and unfolding plan of harmony, love, and peace in the uni- verse, it has all the force and power of creation.

The second principle of manifestation is affirmation. This involves two stages: a discharge, or clearing out of anything that blocks the energy given direction by our act of will; and a recharge, or an energiz- ing of the pattern we wish to accomplish by gathering and committing our resources toward that end. In the house analogy, we can't move beyond the blueprint stage until we remove various obstacles. We have to get the right land use permits. We need to clear the building site of boulders or trees, or the remnants of past structures. We must be sure there are no problems with the utility hook-ups.

Then we have to commit our resources: we have to have the money, the tools, the supplies and materials, the construction crew. We have to energize and support what we have set in motion with all that we have, affirming with our thoughts and actions our intention to complete what we have begun. The affirmation stage is very impor- tant, because challenges to the success of our mission will inevitably arise. Things cost more than we anticipated; the soil is not proper for the drainage required; members of the construction crew find they have to be elsewhere. To fulfill the realization of our hopes, we need to continually reaffirm our intention, seeing the finished state as if it already existed, directing our resources toward that end, and thereby magnetizing what is needed for completion.

Finally, the third principle is purposeful action. We dig the holes, we mix the mortar, we nail the posts, we lay the bricks, and we do this not at random, but on purpose, aligned with the pattern laid out by our intention and affirmed with the flow of our resources. We actualize, with our physical effort and tangible materials, that which we have envisioned.

This process of manifestation, like the river of love, exists whether we are consciously engaged with it or not. In other words, we are always creating our reality. The shape and texture of our lives do not just arbitrarily happen to us; we are co-creators of our circumstances, participants with everyone else in the family of life in constructing the world around and within us.

Most of us recognize without question that our actions shape our lives, but we may fail to understand that the more subtle acts of thought and speech do the same. The mind is the originator; our thoughts connect us with Source. The power of creation unfolds from what we believe, desire, or envision. Our words express and affirm our thoughts. We articulate what has meaning for us, and in doing so we give energy to that meaning. Our emotions or feelings also carry a certain vibration, which we broadcast to those around us, whether consciously or unconsciously.

So body, speech, and mind, we are always shaping our reality and, since we are all interrelated, we are also shaping the shared reality for all our relations. This is a sobering thought, for it means we each carry great responsibility for the world we construct. It is also an empowering thought, for it means we each carry the power or potential to create a world of peace and harmony.

If we can use these principles of manifestation to build a house, so too can we use them to build peace. We activate the ideal of peace through that inner knowing that "there has to be a better way." We affirm our intention to realize that ideal through clearing the obstacles in our relationships—we transcend the "us" and "them" mentality and open our hearts, engaging the reconciliation process. Then we move to action, solving together the problems that are the cause of our conflict and creating systems that will sustain us in our newfound partnerships.

Since we are always creating our reality, individually and collectively, our choices are not about the fact of our participation in that co-creation process, but about its direction and purpose. We are manifesting something in every moment, and since we are always (all ways) in relationship, we are determining the shape and quality of those relationships with every breath. If it is greater peace, serenity, harmony, healing, or reconciliation that we choose to manifest through our activities of thought, word, and deed, then we are peacebuilders in every moment. Or not.

What kinds of action, what skills and approaches can we use to make peace a living reality in our lives? How can we let the Spirit of Peace express itself through us as activity that will bring to fruition the seeds of peace we all carry? How can we truly be peacebuilders in every moment—in our personal lives, in our families, in our workplace and community, in our nation and in the world?

Unleashing the Power of Peace

To address these questions, we need to look at what I call the four C's of peacebuilding: choice, creativity, cooperation, and courage. We will also explore what it takes to build enduring systems of peace, and the power of the individual to make a difference. Finally, we will consider the set of skills involved in risking the action for peace.

What Is Peacebuilding?

We know the term "peacekeeping" from the United Nations' peace-keeping missions around the world. We know the term "peacemaking" because that is the word usually associated with the work of resolving conflicts and spreading peace. "Blessed are the peacemakers" is a familiar phrase from the Bible.

Although I find the word *peacemaking* to be a strong word, I actually prefer *peacebuilding*. To "make" something suggests establishing something new, something that didn't exist before. Peace, however, always and already is. Technically speaking, we don't "make" it, since it inherently exists as our inner template for right relationship. We can, however, build on, build up, increase, or amplify peace.

I also like the image of building. When I was in third grade, my class went on a field trip to observe the construction of a house a few blocks away from school. We watched over many months, as the house grew from its beginning cellar hole to its final landscaping. We had milk and cookies with the new owners, to celebrate their moving in. To this day, nearly fifty years later, I can drive by that house and remember what it looks like from the inside out.

Many years ago, I worked with my husband to design and build our own house. Through this, I came to understand the inner workings of the building process. I see tens if not hundreds of houses every day, and from the outside I can marvel at their various shapes, sizes, and settings. Yet when I think about the steps involved in creating the finished product, I marvel at all that is involved.

Now I know about the need for getting the right permits, clearing the space, laying a strong foundation, and putting up a solid structure that is carefully designed to withhold the inevitable stresses and strains of existence. Now I know about the importance of infrastructure—the interior rods that hold the concrete in place, the wiring and plumbing mazes that travel through the walls and from floor to floor, the distribution of the weight so that no one wall or beam needs to carry more than it safely can.

Now I understand about inner transportation—the need for good flow from one part to the other. I recognize the importance of the right material and design for the roof, so it can protect the inner space from rain and snow. I realize the importance of window placement for good light, and of the subtle qualities of space and shape that confer beauty and warmth, turning a house into a home. Most of all, now I appreciate the process of building, of bringing alive someone's dream, of moving from blueprint to tangible reality.

Building peace is like building a house. Peace exists in the ideal realm, and our job is to bring it into manifestation. Peace, too, needs a strong foundation, an appropriate infrastructure, good protection from bad weather, and all the trimmings and details that ensure its ability to stand for a long, long time, providing a home within which generations of children might grow up safely and happily.

Unleashing the Power of Peace

Choice: I Choose, Therefore I Am

Action begins with choice. With free will, we are making choices all the time. Specifically, we choose to act, or not to act, in certain ways. Sometimes the choices we are called upon to make are not pleasant or easy. Sometimes we have to leap into the realm of faith, because our choices propel us into unknown territory, and we need to trust somehow that they will bring good results even when we can't see the future clearly. Sometimes, we have to choose those actions that we know will bring us a new set of challenges and pressures.

My own life is a testament to the power of choice to set in motion the process of manifestation, indeed, of transformation. When I made the choice, after the second round of cancer, to live every moment full of life, love, joy, and peace, I was aware that I was not doing that just for myself, but to be of service to the world. In other words, my will was aligned with a higher purpose or power.

Over the next several years, I noticed an interesting phenomenon. I found that my choice had an effect similar to sounding a tuning fork in front of an orchestra. Just as every instrument will then be tuned to that note, so over time every part of my being not attuned with my new intention came to the surface for review and transformation. In the whirlwind of that experience, with its many temptations to give up or give in, I discovered the affirmation phase by necessity; that is, I realized I needed to hold to my goal unwaveringly, repeatedly reaffirming my purpose, clearing the obstacles and recommitting my resources. I also found that I needed to act in accordance with the choices I had made. There is no question in my mind that, had I not done all this, I would not be alive today. There is also no question in my mind that the entire process hinged on making that choice, which ultimately brought me to my work as a peacebuilder.

My particular choice was about life and death, but the choice that leads us to act as peacebuilders may be occasioned by several factors. The first step, though, is even to realize that we have choices. Often, our behavior is so conditioned by repetitive and socially conditioned responses that we react automatically, without bothering to assess the endless possibilities for action. Indeed, we always have a choice. Even if someone is pointing a gun to our head, we still can choose how we respond. We may not like the choices that are apparent to us, but they exist. With a little pause for centering home, we might even find new choices we didn't see at first glance.

When my husband and I decided to end our marriage, I remember going through a series of difficult choices, each of which required me to come to terms with a painful reality and realize I had more options than were readily apparent. We had a small child, whose stability we wanted to protect as much as possible in the uprooting of our family life.

My progression of thought went something like this: "I can leave the marriage but I can't leave the house, because that would upset my daughter's routine too much." Then, after some time to digest the implications of that: "OK, I can leave the house but I can't move very far away because my daughter needs to continue to see her father reg-ularly." Then, after some time sitting with that, I got to: "OK, I can move further away, but not so far that I can't keep taking her to the same baby-sitter."

Finally, I realized that I really needed to move to another city, for my own personal and professional well-being, which meant changing all kinds of routines. By then, choices that would have seemed inconceivable only a few weeks previously appeared quite manageable, once I accepted the new circumstances fully and allowed myself to consider the whole range of options. And in fact, my husband and I were able to establish a friendly and effective routine of coparenting between cities that lasted for many years and allowed all of us to take the next steps in our life's journey.

Diana Lion, a Canadian peacebuilder living in Berkeley, California, shares a story about choice.

Imagine sitting in a central concrete basement classroom, fluorescent lights blinking erratically. Groups of men talk as they walk through our classroom, on their way back to their cells. Uniformed and armed guards stroll through once in a while. For prisoners in the "Alternatives to Violence Project" (AVP) this is the most intimate sharing opportunity they have access to in their time in San Quentin.

Many men in our twice-monthly support groups say that they live from AVP to AVP. One evening, an inmate told the AVP circle of having been collared by another prisoner—an act which could, and often does, lead to an escalation of violence, retaliation, stabbing, and extended time in solitary. Instead of rising to the threat, he stepped back and paused. During that pause he realized he had choices, and he was able to transform that moment away from being a potentially fatal one. He walked away, spent some time alone, and later went to talk with the other man. He said that what he had practiced at AVP had made that shift possible.

This man was able to overcome a familiar response pattern because he had learned about a better way. We can all do this, even though it is difficult. Sometimes, our conditioning is so strong, that we keep repeating our accustomed behavior, despite growing evidence that it is not having the effect we desire. We might even escalate the response, doing it more loudly or strongly, in the misguided assumption that, since we haven't gotten what we want yet, it must be because "they" haven't heard us.

I remember walking in to a meeting room in a Palestinian dialogue center, and seeing a great adage on the wall. It said, "If you always do what you always did, you always get what you always got." This saying has become like a mantra for me in peacebuilding situations, as over and over again I notice people continuing to act in the same, tired, ineffectual ways, as if sooner or later they will prevail by sheer force of will. Protracted negotiations in such places as Northern Ireland, the Middle East, Cyprus, and elsewhere, however, have shown us that until people are willing to look at alternatives to their established and favored positions, they will not be able to arrive at a peaceful conclusion to their conflict.

Maggi Cage, a Wisconsin peacebuilder, tells of how she was able to change her habitual behavior to find a new set of choices.

I had been involved in the antiwar protests during the '60s, very committed to that style of attempting to make peace in a war situation. When the Persian Gulf War came along, it seemed to me that doing the same thing we did in the '60s just wasn't the right thing to do anymore. I couldn't go out and create more hostility in the process of advocating for peace; it just didn't seem to make any sense. But on the other hand, I couldn't just do nothing, and not make some expression of my displeasure with the Persian Gulf War.

So for me it really was an internal process of asking a different kind of question. Rather than asking, "How can I oppose the war?", the question came to my mind, "How can I make peace in a world that is experiencing war at this moment? What is something that I can do to create more peace in the world?" The answer was very clear to me, and it was to get pro-life and pro-choice people in the abortion debate to talk to each other, because that was a part of warring in the world that I was directly experiencing. So it really came out of that "Ah-ha" for me, to ask a different question. This led me to talk with a mediator friend and form the first dialogue group in Wisconsin on the abortion issue.

Actually, the choice Maggi made is a common one among activists, who have found over the years that the energy of working for something positive is more effective than, or at least as important as, working against something negative. Certainly, if we are creating our reality by how we direct our energy, then by opposing something we are actually subtly feeding it, and many of us have had the experience of seeing our protests simply strengthen the resolve of the other side. Oppositional or adversarial approaches sustain the "us" versus "them" mentality and hurt the possibility for developing understanding and joint approaches to shared problems. Does this mean we should allow actions that we consider morally wrong to pass unnoticed; that we should not speak out against injustice? No, but it may mean we need to widen our range of responses to include building something new together.

Creativity: Expanding the Possibilities

When people are in conflict, or are not at peace with one another, whether in a work situation, a love relationship, or between historical "enemies," there are issues between them that are unresolved. To address these issues successfully, we need to get creative about what is possible. Too often, we simply make demands about how the other should change, or should act the way we want them to, or should "fix" their wrong behavior or attitude, as if making such demands will solve the problems. It won't.

Conflicts often reach a point of deadlock or stalemate, as each side wants its own solution imposed on the situation. Even if parties realize they may need to compromise, they may do so in a way that splits the difference between them, usually ending up vaguely (or acutely) dissatisfied with the outcome.

As long as conflicting parties see themselves in a face-off against each other, with the notion that one will "win" by outsmarting, out-negotiating, overpowering, or simply tiring out the other, there is no room for peace to grow. A compromise does not necessarily change the basic structure of the situation—"us" against "them." What's needed instead is the realization that the issues between people are an occasion for common cause. That is, they can join together to face the problems they share, seeking solutions that work for everyone.

For instance, loggers and environmentalists may see themselves as "opponents" on the issue of cutting in an old-growth forest. If they compromise, by agreeing on certain limits to the amount of trees cut, they have not really addressed the core problem, nor changed the basic adversarial nature of the relationship. Nor have they satisfied the interests of either side in any sustainable way. By working together to create new forest-related jobs that are environment-friendly, however, they would be laying the foundation for a whole new way of addressing the problem, and each other.

Once this basic shift is made in how the conflict is framed, the possibilities for peace are limited only by our own imaginations. I find that the single greatest resource for solving difficult problems is our creative imagination. After all, if these problems were easy to solve, we would have done so already. We need to go into the zone of our minds where we have access to other ways of understanding, learning, and perceiving, in order to open ourselves to the vast wisdom potential of our nature, and to draw from that pool of possibility the unique suggestions that will work in each circumstance.

When I speak of a zone in our minds, I mean the area of the right brain, where we have access to poetry, intuition, metaphor, and other nonlinear ways of accessing and expressing information and meaning. Some people can tap into their creative mode easily; others may be more at home in the reasoning, logical functions of the brain. That's one of the advantages of people working together to solve their problems—we can use the resources of the larger whole rather than depend on any one of us to find new approaches.

Pete Swanson, a mediator based in Washington, D.C., learned at his mother's knee the imperative of expanding the options, and a simple method for doing so.

When I was a child, my mother always told me, "Pete, in any situation in which you find a problem or a challenge, make yourself think of seven different ways to solve the problem, and from there you will find one that works. However, you must challenge yourself to always find seven!"

Now, I never forgot this, even when I wanted to. It haunts me as a mediator, because I find myself constantly challenging parties to come up with seven different ways to address the disagreements before them. In one situation, I was to train a particular government team in negotiation skills. At the end of the training, we had to find a way to bring closure to the events of the week, so I said to myself, "What is an appropriate way to cap off this training?" Of course, my mother popped into my head, and her words rang out, clear as day. "Have each one of them come up with seven different, concrete ways they can put this training to use." Following that guidance, I gave them their task, and before we knew it we had a list of well over 150 ways they could implement these skills to make a tangible difference back home!

The Metaphoric Third Force

Whether I work in ethnic conflicts around the world, or with individuals, families, or organizations in the United States, I like to invite people into the realm of creativity, and, more particularly, into the realm of metaphor to expand the options they perceive between them. Metaphor is a way of accessing universal or archetypal truths through symbols, comparisons, analogies, and images. It is also an impersonal space that acts as what I call "the third force."

Imagine two people pushing against each other. They can push back and forth indefinitely, or until one or the other tires or gains outside support to bolster their cause. The force that each one exerts is directed toward the other, and the force that each one receives is met and matched by a return push. In other words, the relationship is stuck; it goes nowhere. I picture this as a straight line, with the energy going from the two outer points toward the middle.

If, however, there were another force brought into the situation—a force that turned the attention of the two parties away from each other directly and toward a third point in what now becomes a triangle—the parties become free to work together with and toward that other point. The energy, instead of being stuck in the middle of a line, can now flow around the triangle in all directions.

Many things can act as a third force. For me, metaphor is one of the strongest, because it is universally accessible. For instance, I remember a time when I was working with a group of peacebuilders in Bosnia. We were working with the skills of peacebuilding through the metaphor of gardening, talking about the peacebuilder as the gardener who must prepare the soil, clear away the weeds, carefully select the appropriate plants, and nurture them through many seasons. Everyone can appreciate this set of generic behaviors.

Within the framework of this metaphor, participants were able to go in and out of discussing some of the most painful aspects of their war experiences, because they were protected by the metaphor. That is, in being able to talk about hatred as a weed, or hope as a tender seedling, or a wave of ethnic cleansing as a storm, they were able to address deep and difficult issues with the kind of distance and safety needed to make such a discussion possible so soon after the traumatic events in their lives.

Metaphors come in many forms. Some are visual images, like the mountain of lies I wrote of earlier. People who are good at visualizing will naturally "see" a mountain in their mind's eye when they hear that metaphor. Other metaphors are more body-centered. I will never forget a workshop with Turkish Cypriots, when I asked two people to demonstrate a true partnership relationship. The two men stood side by side and leaned their shoulders against each other, putting more and more weight on the point where their shoulders met, until their bodies were at a sharp angle to one another, like an inverted V. Holding each other up in that way (had either moved aside, the other would have fallen down), they walked down the center of the room. No words could have said more about partnership.

Mary Jacksteit runs dialogue groups on the abortion issue between pro-life and pro-choice adherents. She asks people at the end of the session to offer a metaphor describing their experience. She shares two of these: "When I was growing up, we lived on a farm. There was one long grassy hill that we kids liked to roll down. It was full of clover. But there were bees in the clover, and I was always afraid to roll down for fear of getting stung. Today was like that. I wanted to roll down the clover hillside, but was afraid of the bees. But I did roll down, and I didn't get stung."

"This workshop felt to me like a wall of icky slime that I was being asked to thrust my hand into. I didn't want to do it. But what I found was that when I did reach in my hand, I felt another hand from the other side clasping mine."

Into the Zone

Moving into metaphor is only one creative way to advance our understanding or our problem solving. There are many others entry points into the zone of creativity, where ideas and images arise seemingly from nowhere and carry us into new associations and insights. This zone is simply a doorway to our deeper resources, the pool of infinite potential in which we all have our essential being. Tapping that source ensures that we will arrive at unique solutions to our problems.

I am reminded of Djidja, a peacebuilder I know in Bosnia. Her town was besieged by enemy troops for three years. That's three years of shells falling on buildings and byways, of snipers sitting on hilltops, picking off people exposed in their yards or streets. Obviously, normal life was impossible. People spent long hours and days in hallways or basements, makeshift shelters that offered at least minimal protection against flying glass, sniper bullets, or shrapnel.

Under these circumstances, the situation of the young children was particularly distressing. Cooped up for long periods of time in cramped quarters, unable to exercise their growing bodies or minds, afraid for their lives, the children suffered greatly. Djidja was a teacher who realized she needed creative ways of keeping the children engaged in their "work," which was learning. She developed a series of radio programs that she was able to broadcast locally. In these programs, she offered the children a variety of stories, games, and lessons that they could do in the shelters. Her voice and her invitation to the children to participate in the games were a lifeline for many families during those difficult years.

Sometimes, a creative response is something that is unexpected or unfamiliar. When someone receives a message that they are not prepared for, or that jolts them into another frame of reference, there is a moment of cognitive dissonance, when the heart and mind are open to new possibilities. Patricia Deer, who mediates employee discrimination cases, has a story about such a moment.

One of my most interesting cases concerned an African American janitor who worked for the city government of a medium-sized town. He had worked long years for the city, and over those years he had applied for many promotions. Most recently, the city had deemed him unqualified for a supervisory level position and hired a white man from the outside. He filed a discrimination suit against the city based on race.

The case came to mediation. During the mediation he sat across the table from two city officials. He wanted education to help him qualify for a promotion. The officials said they were not obligated to do anything. They were confident that they had made a decision on merits, and would not be liable in an investigation for discrimination. They showed no interest in accommodation. There was simply a friendly stone wall.

These kinds of mediations always use a private caucus with each party. During my caucus with the city officials, they used tactful words to describe a person considered by them to be much too "uppity." But their description of him sounded to me like a person with leadership qualities. I suddenly blurted out the question, "You mean like John Kennedy?" They looked at me in surprise; what did I mean? I explained that they seemed to be describing a person with vision and courage, giving them a new and unexpected lens to look through. They got it. They ended up giving him everything he had asked for.

As we wrote up the agreement, they asked me if I was related to the Kennedys. They wondered where that insight came from. Their question confirmed for me that my comparison of the janitor and John Kennedy, as unlikely as it may have seemed, had created a shift. I inwardly marveled at the gift of the right word at the right time, with no blame or shame attached.

Sometimes creativity is nothing more than going beneath the surface of the obvious, probing for more information. I am reminded of the classic story of two children who each clamor to have the one orange in the house. The mother, thinking she is solving the problem, cuts the orange in half. When the children continue to be upset, she is at a loss. Only when she takes the time to explore the reasons why each child wanted the orange, does she find what could have been an alternative solution. One child wanted the juice of the orange to drink; the other wanted the rind to make a cake. They could each have easily had all of what they wanted, had anyone been able to look beyond compromise.

I think of Rawda, a Palestinian speech therapist who, having survived eight years in an Israeli prison, returned to her community with a profound commitment to stop the suffering she had experienced so deeply. She soon found herself taking a most unusual route to fulfill her purpose. As part of an Israeli peace effort, an American woman went to Rawda's town to teach Reiki, a Japanese form of energy healing. Rawda learned the method, and began to use it in her clinic, even though this was a totally new and strange approach in her society.

The results have been astounding. Children and their mothers have experienced deep healing through this process. Now, more than 200 Palestinians have learned Reiki, and Rawda and others are trained to teach it. This most unlikely of approaches from a distant land has become state-of-the-art healing technology in Rawda's town.

Marcia Kreisel, part of the Israeli peace iniative that brought Reiki to Rawda's community, reports on what she witnessed:

> On one of my visits to Rawda's clinic, I saw a ten-year-old boy who had been brought in by his mother. The boy's father had recently been taken to prison by Israeli soldiers, and the boy had witnessed the soldiers breaking into the house, beating his father and breaking things. When I saw him, he was in a state of absolute terror, screaming and running, banging into walls in an effort to get out. Rawda sat down and raised her hands to send Reiki, and at the same time began singing him a lullaby.
>
> Two months later, I was again at the clinic, and the same boy was there. This time he was sprawled on a treatment table, with a smile of great pleasure on his face, waiting to receive his Reiki—and with total trust, he also let me give him Reiki. You can imagine the joy I felt as I experienced the healing of this child.

Cooperation: When We Work Together

If creativity is the doorway through which we can reach into the infinite realm of potential and draw to us creative options for solving our problems, then cooperation is the vehicle that can carry us to community. Cooperation is what allows the broken threads of relationship to be rewoven into the whole fabric of caring and sharing. Working together for a common goal, helping one another, connecting us in our efforts to find a better way—this is the basic ground of peacebuilding in our homes and in our offices, in our communities and between countries.

Cooperation sounds like a no-brainer. Of course, when we can work together, we can accomplish far more than any of us can alone. Yet all the institutions of our society—our schools, our businesses, our political system—reward competitiveness and individualism, while authoritarian families and hierarchical organizations teach us that the power of decision making rests in the individual, not in the collective. No wonder we don't know how to cooperate very well.

When I give people simple group activities to do together, and even when I speak beforehand of the value of cooperation and describe cooperative behaviors, it is still extremely difficult for people to figure out how to share resources, not compete for air time or leadership, and learn to use the collective mind. Repeatedly, I watch people unable to complete a simple task or solve a simple puzzle because they are unable to work together.

At the same time, when people do make the breakthrough, and realize that by pooling their energy and information they can accomplish their task and even go beyond it, they are so excited and pleased, as if they have discovered something new and precious in their lives. That's because cooperation seems to increase our sense of aliveness and empowerment.

We are all familiar with examples of how, in crises, people pull together and help one another out. Some time ago there was a severe ice storm in the Northeast, and people went without electricity, in some cases, for days and weeks. Afterward, many people reported that they were sorry to see the electricity come on again, because during that time they had had to rely on their neighbors, caring for and supporting one another in ways that they never had before. While stories like these are inspiring and heartwarming, they also point out how unfamiliar we have become, in our modern industrial society, with cooperation as a way of life.

Jonathan Reitman, a lawyer-mediator from Brunswick, Maine, tells of a time in his legal practice when the switch to a cooperative mode eased a tense labor–management standoff and averted possible violence.

Several years ago, I was the lawyer for the 7,500 unionized production workers at a large manufacturing facility. As in most unionized workplaces, the issue of subcontracting work to "outside" non-union contractors was always highly controversial. On this day, the issue had boiled over, resulting in a "wildcat strike" that put thousand of workers on the street.

The union always maintained that to subcontract out "bargaining unit work" was a violation of the collective bargaining agreement, and "took food off the plates of our children." Management frequently responded, as they had in this instance, that the work in question could not be performed by members of the production union without disrupting schedules and diverting resources from other tasks. In other words, management said, we had no choice but to subcontract.

The battle lines were drawn at the start of the morning shift when thousand of employees walked off the job and gathered outside the union hall across the street. Throughout the day, confrontational negotiations were conducted sporadically. Accusations of illegality and bad faith flew back and forth across the bargaining table. I monitored these polarized discussions from my office. With no progress reported, I headed home, where I received a call around

Unleashing the Power of Peace

11 P.M. from the union president. He explained that talks were still stalemated, and asked whether I could join the negotiation.

When I arrived at the facility, the first person I saw was my counterpart, the attorney for management, for whom I had deep respect despite our differing loyalties. The first thing he said was, "Jon, we have a problem." That simple statement totally reframed the debate. All day long each side had been accusing each other of being the cause of the problem. My colleague's statement transformed the situation into a shared problem that required the collaboration of both sides to solve.

Within three hours, both parties found a way to save face and negotiate an acceptable compromise. Without my adversary's conciliatory opening and my ability to see the potential it created, this labor dispute, like so many others, would surely have had a different outcome.

My own lessons in cooperation grew from the opportunities presented by being a single mother, newly divorced, and sick with cancer—hardly a happy scenario. Yet the very desperateness of my situation required me to find help. There was no way I could have managed my life in that state without the cooperation of many friends. Though that help came in many forms, one that was most meaningful to me was the opportunity to live in a household with other adults and children, where we were responsible together for the healthy functioning of the whole. In addition, I knew other single moms and dads, and we found ways to help each other with the inevitable challenges of single parenting.

From that experience, I learned that the most important skill within cooperation is the skill of trusting that one's own needs will be met by addressing the needs of others. This takes faith, and a willingness to both give and receive. It requires a letting go into the larger whole, and having confidence that one is held safely in that web.

The shift to a cooperative mode has begun to take hold in some parts of the business community. Whereas previously companies were arranged in separate, isolated, and even competitive departments, the necessities of a global market require that different parts of a single company work together seamlessly. This has occasioned a significant effort at relearning for many workers, and particularly for managers, as teamwork within and across departments and even companies has become necessary for success.

Gail West, a consultant and education in Taiwan, reports on work she and her colleagues have done in major corporations, assisting in this relearning process.

> A particular machine tool company was not quite making its targets year after year. Though poised for rapid financial growth, the company was stuck in complacency.
>
> The Managing Director, Mr. S., saw a dangerous plateau. Internally the company was compartmentalized, with each department working in isolation for its own benefit, and sometimes at cross-purposes with other departments. Teamwork was sporadic, leadership was autocratic and centralized, and systems haphazard. All of this meant that customers' needs went unmet. A team of outside consultants came in to help the employees focus on new possibilities, through a series of participatory group dialogues and planning programs.

Mr. S. was a very bright, fast, driving leader. Members of his management team knew from many years of experience that if they waited, he would make the decisions, relieving them of responsibility. During the participatory planning programs, the facilitators suggested that he might restrain his verbal brilliance so as to open the space for others to step forward. When he did so, his teammates were shocked! All of them then had to make a new decision about their relationships to each other, their own leadership role, and the organization.

With constant encouragement, Mr. S. continued holding back, though it was difficult for him, until regular team dialogue sessions and a cooperative culture were established, where individuals felt safe enough to express themselves honestly and were respected for their participation. One employee described this type of cooperation as "the most powerful tool for pulling down barriers between departments and people, resulting in mutual trust with management." Another reported that the participatory approach accounted for "the revival of spirit and enthusiasm in the organization."

In the words of Mr. S., "It is a continuous journey, a journey with a shifting goal line; once one is on that journey, the commitment increases and accelerates. People have a tremendous potential that is just waiting to be unleashed through opportunities for participation and cooperation."

Finding Common Ground

I have seen many situations where people who were deeply engaged in hostile, adversarial, or competitive relationships were able to change almost magically into allies, simply from having a chance to be heard. We all need the respect that comes with being acknowledged, and having our voice and our views included. When our participation is invited and our ideas honored, we are often willing to step toward our former adversary to see what we might do together. In fact, we are even able to discover common goals or values that we never knew existed before.

One place where this dynamic has become most evident is in dealing with ideological conflicts. Conflicts can be over many things: resources, identity, power, ideas, information. Those in which we argue about our belief systems are the hardest to resolve, because we are affirming the "truth" of our truths against those who believe something entirely different. The abortion debate in America is one example of such a contentious situation. Passions are high on both sides; moral imperatives are declared; religious beliefs are held inviolable. Unfortunately, the war of words has escalated, and extremist behavior, including violence, has become a sad part of the conversation.

In such a conflict, it is not possible to compromise or to negotiate a mutually acceptable outcome: the parties will not convince the other side of the rightness of their cause. However, when they can come together in dialogue, and take that step toward the other in understanding, people have found a new level of common ground and a creative way to cooperate. In one case I know of, the two sides agreed that they shared a common value, namely a desire to see a lower rate of teen pregnancies. With that agreement, they were able to work together in a project that addressed teen pregnancies without touching on the subject of abortion.

Other issues beside ideological disputes are rending our social and political fabric. Our particular brand of democracy insures that for every public policy issue, there are a wide variety of voices. Environmental concerns, tax policies, health care, crime, education, political leadership—these are the types of issues that, on a local, state, and national level citizens are contending over on a regular basis. Our racial and economic differences add further spice to the mix.

Eileen Babbitt, a professor at the Fletcher School of Law and Diplomacy at Tufts University, tells of a group she once worked with in a city trying to promote harmony among its various ethnic populations and deal with its many urban problems.

> We met for four days with a group of civic leaders from the white, Asian, Hispanic, and African American communities. At first, they explored their needs, concerns, and fears. This was a powerful event, as many people shared personal experiences where they felt misunderstood, unsupported or hurt by those from other groups.
>
> With so many problems in the city, the group decided to focus on their joint concern about growing youth violence. Their efforts at finding common ground on how to approach this problem led them to a commitment to strengthen local leadership opportunities for people of color, thereby giving minority-group youth some hope for their own future and a greater sense of ownership in the life of the community.
>
> In the discussion of leadership, one African American woman told of a time she had decided to run for a seat on the mostly all-white school board. Eminently qualified, with lots of experience, exposure, and credibility in her own community, she felt terribly let down when she lost the election, especially realizing that the sup-

port she had expected from the other minority groups had not been forthcoming. She felt her experience of stepping forward to provide leadership had been so humiliating that she vowed never to subject herself or her family to that again.

Over the ensuing days, the discussion turned to a consideration of possible action steps to address the leadership issue. Soon, the discussion faltered, and the group felt a sense of discouragement and stalemate. A pattern had emerged: whenever someone of color would make a suggestion, one of the white participants would counter with reasons why it wouldn't work. The minority groups then naturally interpreted that as the whites blocking their empowerment and refusing to support their aspirations; the whites thought they were actually being helpful, alerting the people to the pitfalls and realities in the system. This kind of cross-communication, full of untested assumptions and growing animosity, was an all-too-familiar example of what had happened over years of civic life, deeply embedding the various groups in their negative convictions about the "other."

When this pattern was identified, the energy shifted dramatically. Once their experience was truly named, the participants could turn their attention to finding some new ways to interact. At that point, the African American woman who had run for school committee shared that she was beginning to revisit her decision never to run again. She knew she had a strong desire to help her community and her city, but still had a fear of the "stone wall" phenomenon and lack of support she had experienced before. Recognizing her previous experience as a mini-version of the dynamic that was being played out and described in the group, she offered a challenge: she would run again if the group would support her.

This challenge gave the group the opportunity to do things differently—and cooperatively. Rather than simply say Yes in the passion of the moment, and then do nothing, people gave realistic assessments of their willingness and ability to support her candidacy. Some had already made commitments to other candidates; others were not sure where they stood. But all considered what they reasonably could and couldn't do, given their constraints and desires. In the end, a white woman from the group became her campaign manager, an Hispanic American man and an Asian American woman became organizers for her campaign in their communities, and others helped in other ways.

She won the election. Most of the workshop participants were present at her victory celebration, where they expressed great pride in their joint accomplishment, and where she joyfully acknowledged she couldn't have done it without their support, both in the workshop and in the election campaign.

Courage: Peace Is Not for Wimps

I was in Jerusalem when Yitzchak Rabin was assassinated, and I had the opportunity to go through the first round of shock and mourning with the Israeli people. One of the biggest lessons for me in those days was the realization that making peace can often be more difficult than making war. It can also be dangerous. This is not an activity for the faint of heart. Peacebuilding is an act of courage, as we confront, in ourselves and in each other, all that keeps us from walking with the Spirit of Peace.

Yiota, a Greek Cypriot involved in peacebuilding activities in Cyprus, expresses this more beautifully than I ever could.

> The road of peace is the hardest one. I believe in peace because I am a mother, and as my children are getting older, I become stronger in this feeling. I feel that to choose the road of peace is the most difficult and full of obstacles, because it means that I have to accept you, and I have to do inner work to accept you. I have to sit down and have a battle with my own self. I have to see who I am, with my strengths and weaknesses. I have to be willing to transform myself in order to accept and respect the difference between you and me. This is the most difficult thing. Otherwise I hate you, I dismiss you, I shut my heart and I think I'm safe, by continuing my own way and excluding you from my life. That's why I think the road of peace is the hardest one.
>
> I don't want my children or any other children of this world to suffer the bitterness of a war. War traumas never heal because there is no fair war, and it is not fair for all those lives to be wasted. If someone comes now and tells me, "Give your life; you will die, but we guarantee that nobody in the future will have a war or kill each other," I can do it.

The word *courage* comes from the French word for "heart." The courage to act in the face of danger, to reach out through the blur of hatred, to witness for peace and justice, and above all to love in the face of fear—these are acts of the heart. Courage is what happens when love and action meet in the heart. Because we love, because we care, because we want to relieve suffering or see something better for our children—because our hearts are filled and overflowing with the longing for the Spirit of Peace to inhabit our lives, we do what needs to be done.

During the time when I was healing from cancer, and walking that edge between life and death, people used to say to me that I had great courage. By that they meant that I was somehow noble or brave. I would respond, "No, I'm not brave; I'm just doing what I need to do in order to heal." When we need to act for peace, in spite of the consequences, in spite of the effort, in spite of the threats and challenges, the fullness of our hearts is feeding our actions, and we are unstoppable.

Yitzchak Rabin was unstoppable. He did not start out as a peacemaker in the traditional sense. He was a warrior. In Native American history, the terms "peace path" and "war path" were not metaphors but real roads, to be traveled according to one's intention. When one who has walked the war path, as did Yitzchak Rabin, crosses over to the peace path, much effort is involved. He entered the peace path reluctantly at first, and, once convinced that it was the best and only way for his people, he stayed the course. And he died with "peace" (in Hebrew, *shalom*) on his lips, literally.

Rabin left this life in a moment of very high energy, surrounded by tens of thousands of people expressing their love and support for him and his march toward peace. He went out after publicly embracing his longtime political rival-turned-peace partner, Shimon Peres. Earlier, he had shaken hands with his avowed "enemy," Yasser Arafat. He went out shortly after singing a song of peace. All this for a man, who, we are told, did not easily display nor receive affection, who never sang, whose own difficult journey toward peace was personal and harshly political, not arising from the comforting community and shared passions of a popular movement.

For me, Rabin, like Anwar Sadat before him, exemplified the courage for peace, but not because they were killed for their actions. For me, these men are symbols of courage because, as Yiota reminds us, they went through their own transformation process, and brought forth the results as an offering to humanity. They did what needed to be done to make the incredible shift that could begin a bridging of the deep chasm in the Middle East. They did it first within themselves, and then presented themselves to lead their people through the unknown and terrifying wilderness toward peace, a journey that would require many deaths and rebirths, inner and outer, at the individual and collective levels.

I use this imagery reminiscent of the flight of the Hebrews out of Egypt to the Promised Land deliberately. What Moses, Sadat, and Rabin showed us was simply the extreme of what each one of us may go through if we are to live as vehicles for the Spirit of Peace. To be a peacebuilder in every moment is to travel some version of the heroic journey.

The heroic journey is the journey of transformation. We begin by acknowledging that this journey is not a simple one, like going to the market for milk, but is a quest, a spiritual process by which we discover the Holy Grail, or the whole and holy nature of our own humanity. On our quest we are tested; we meet the monster in the road. That monster is crafted by our minds, stuffed with our loss and suffering, our fear and bitterness, our intolerance and prejudice, our "enemy" projections of the "other," our illusion of separation.

Our test is to slay the dragon, not through force and battle, but by seeing it for what it really is—a monster of our own creation. When we name its true name, and are willing to go into the heart of the beast, we abandon ourselves to the unknown, and die to the world as we know it. We give ourselves over to the possibility of understanding and compassion, of healing and reconciliation, and in that we allow some significant shift to occur in our lives, a shift that, once made, means we can never again be as we were before.

Having made this shift, we complete the heroic journey by bringing the gift or boon of our learning back to others. We act for peace because something has changed in us; because we have survived our encounter with evil or separation, and have found the strength and courage to declare for peace.

This all sounds very high-minded and grandiose, but in fact it is quite mundane. All of us, in choosing greater harmony in our inner life, in a personal relationship, in a work setting, in our communities or in our world, go through some mini-version of this journey. Our tests come in many shapes and sizes. Some we pass, some we need to repeat again and again. That's how it is, and that's OK. Each time we open the heart a little bit more, or take a little bit more personal responsibility for the consequences of how we treat ourselves and each other, we take another step on the journey.

I could fill this book and several others with tales of the test, where people displayed courage in the face of danger and injustice. There is something about the challenge to our very souls that calls forth our power and passion for peace. When put to the ultimate test, where we have to say Yes or No, clearly and immediately, we may feel the adrenaline rush that soldiers report on the battlefield, or crisis workers in emergencies. In that moment, we are warriors for peace.

Of the many stories I could share to illustrate this courage for peace, I have chosen one that I find inspiring because of its very simplicity. It is a story that could be anyone's story, on whatever scale we face that choice, a tale of people doing what needed to be done.

In 1992, my organization brought a group of Greek and Turkish Cypriots off the island of Cyprus for our first bi-communal training program in conflict resolution. The group went to a conference center in England for ten days of skill development and dialogue. This was at a time when very few meetings between the two sides were happening, and when such a meeting could mean being branded a traitor for consorting with the "enemy." Some individuals with high visibility and strong credibility in their communities were in attendance.

When they got home, the Greek Cypriot participants found themselves facing an intense media attack. Cameras and microphones pushed into their faces, they were challenged to explain their treacherous acts. They were accused of many untrue things in newspaper articles, television shows, and radio programs. Some received threatening phone calls, with intimations that their jobs were not secure, that their children were not safe.

After a brief period of confusion, the group rallied their response. They decided to face into the attack rather than to try to run from it. They held a press conference, went on television and radio, and allowed themselves to be interviewed, to counter the false accusations and tell the truth of their own experience. Led by a high-profile woman politician, whose personal credibility and power acted like the bird who flies at the point of the V in a migrating flock, taking the force of the wind to open the way for those behind, they stood firmly in the maelstrom and simply shared what they had learned about peacebuilding, about themselves and the "other."

This act of public courage brought the shift they had made personally into a larger arena. By making their experience known to the public, they opened the doors to a larger citizen peacebuilding process, and made it thinkable and attractive for others, people who might never had considered the possibility before, to step forward as peacebuilders.

Both before and after that time, many committed peacebuilders—both Turkish Cypriot and Greek Cypriot—have shown similar acts of courage. As a result, there is now a large and growing citizens' movement for peacebuilding in Cyprus, actively involving hundreds of citizens from all walks of life in bi-communal meetings for rapprochement and joint action (when such meetings are not shut down for political reasons). While I credit the actions of every single person who has participated in this movement, I believe that this early public, courageous stand by that small group of pioneers laid a cornerstone in the foundation upon which the house of peace is being built, brick by brick, in Cyprus.

People display the courage for peace in many ways. Some are in the foreground; others may be acting less visibly in the background. Some take action on their own; others encourage the actions of others. I consider those who sustain international or local efforts for peace and justice with emotional, financial, and spiritual support, for instance, to be every bit as much a peacebuilder as those who do the practical hands-on work.

Those who witness for peace, testifying by their compassionate presence or their calls for right action, are also courageous peace-builders. One man I know cannot get a job because he refuses to stop saying that the conflict in his country should cease. Another spent months in jail for simply drinking coffee with people from the other side. Amnesty International and other human rights groups have been able to secure the release of many prisoners of conscience, prevent violence, and raise the consciousness of the world about situations of repression, simply by witnessing to what is wrong in our treatment of one another.

When I think of the kind of courage displayed by all who are willing to put their personal safety and well-being on the line for peace, either as a witness or through more direct action, I think ultimately of faith. What allows me to do what I do is the unwavering certainty I hold that peace is possible—indeed, inevitable. This faith is the fire that burns at the meeting point of love and action where courage is born; it is the voice of the Spirit of Peace whispering in our hearts.

One Person Can Make a Difference

Very often, people will ask me how I can possibly hold such a commitment to peace in the face of the overwhelming pain, conflict, and strife in the world. What they're really asking is, "Is it possible for one person to make a real difference?" Underneath this question is a sense that it's all just too big, too much to take on, and that any one individual action is too small to have significant meaning.

In answer, I describe my "drop in the bucket" theory of peacebuilding. I imagine in front of me a big, empty bucket. This is the hole in humanity's heart that allows us to hate and hurt one another, forgetting our inherent wisdom about right relationship and our interconnectedness. I sit with this bucket, and I hold in my hand one small drop of water. This represents a thought, a word, an action that I might take to heal that hole. My drop may seem infinitesimally small compared to the yawning hollow in the bucket, but it is what I have to offer.

I now have a choice what to do with my drop. I can put it into the bucket, or I can cast it aside, with the thought that it doesn't matter anyway so why bother. If I keep choosing to put every drop that comes into my hand into the bucket, and others do so as well (perhaps being influenced by seeing me), then eventually the bucket will fill up and spill over. If I choose to withhold my drop, and others also do that, the bucket will never fill. I cannot choose for others, but I can choose for myself.

Our individual drops are powerful. One drop attracts another, they bind together and build on each other, they create a critical mass. In this way, we are each responsible for building peace in our lives and in the world, for we each have some drop we can offer. When we believe that someone else controls the faucet that fills or empties the bucket, we collude in the fantasy of our own helplessness.

But we are not helpless. I have witnessed many examples of individuals whose single drop has set in motion a whole chain of events supporting peace. I think of a Catholic priest I met, who many years ago went and lived on the streets in a big city, in order to bring his mission of healing to child prostitutes and teenage drug abusers. His efforts led to the founding of a series of centers where young people could get away from the street life and turn their lives around.

I recently read a newspaper story about a twelve-year-old boy from Texas, who felt so strongly about the unresolved conflicts between

Christians, Muslims, and Jews dating back to Crusader times, and especially about the harm caused by the Christian Crusaders during that era, that he embarked on a reconciliation walk. Retracing the steps of the Crusaders from Germany through the Middle East, he shared the message of apology with those he met along the way. Hundreds of people joined him in this walk.

Finally, I think of the people who originated Alcoholics Anonymous, Mothers Against Drunken Driving, and other such movements to address important social issues. These were individuals motivated by their own experiences, deciding to do something about it so others would not have to suffer what they had.

We could all, I am sure, fill books and books with such examples. The point is that we are not helpless—we carry the power to change the world. The question is not, "Do we have the power?" The question is, "How do we use that power for peacebuilding?"

Many years ago, I directed a holistic health program for elders that sponsored a one-day Elders' Celebration. More than 200 senior citizens came, some from nursing homes, some who were living independently. For the opening session, a colleague of mine had arranged for a belly dancer to provide the entertainment. I was appalled! Mostly, I thought it was unfair to ask people with mild to serious health and mobility challenges to watch such a public display of physical grace and strength.

I watched the audience carefully during the performance. Once I realized how much people were enjoying the show—smiling and swaying with the music, and cheering the dancer on—I stopped worrying and turned my attention to the dance. I too enjoyed watching this lovely woman move so beautifully. I noticed that her movements were all spirals, as if she were making figure 8s with the different parts of her body. It even occurred to me that this type of movement must be massaging and cleansing all her internal organs, and that therefore she must be very healthy. I did notice one place in her body, however, that did not seem as flexible—the sternum area. So I wondered if maybe, just maybe, she occasionally got a chest cold.

In the few minutes between the end of her performance and the beginning of my address to the group, I took the time to congratulate her. Then I risked asking a personal question. "Excuse me," I said. "Would you mind telling me, do you ever get sick?" "No," she replied, "almost never, though I do occasionally get a chest cold."

Then I was up front. Somehow I needed to make a bridge between the belly dancing we had all just witnessed and the rest of our celebration time together. As I looked around the room, I realized what I wanted to say. "In this room," I said, "we have the whole continuum of physical flexibility, from grandmother here in her wheelchair, severely crippled with arthritis, all the way to our belly dancer, who can move practically every part of her body with complete ease. Yet for all those differences in ability, each of us in this room, no matter our age or physical condition, has one thing in common. We can all stretch and loosen our bodies just a little bit more.

"Grandmother can work to stretch out her fingers or wiggle her toes; the belly dancer can work to become more flexible in her sternum area. It doesn't matter what our particular stretch is. What matters is that we can each take the next step in flexibility that's right for us."

This awareness holds true for peacebuilding as well. Whoever we are, whatever our life circumstances, we can each take the next step in peacebuilding that's right for us.

Unleashing the Power of Peace: Risking the Action

I have the privilege of knowing a remarkable peacebuilder from the Galilee, a Palestinian-Israeli Melkite priest, Abuna (Father) Chacour. I once heard him give a talk on the Beatitudes, particularly "Blessed are the Peacemakers, for they shall be called the children of God." His interpretation of that injunction, or at least my memory of it, has stayed with me for many years. He said it was really a call to action. As beings made in the image of God, we are by our very nature makers and builders of peace, so what are we waiting for? He said the line really meant, "Get up! Get going! Do something!"

Risking the action for peace means exactly that. Each of us can step forward and risk doing something, whatever our piece is. I use the word *risk* because, like many of the peacebuilders whose stories we have heard, we must be willing to stretch beyond our comfort zone toward peace, without any assurance of the outcome. We must be willing to take the risk of change, and we must be willing for our actions to make a difference.

Often, when people hear my stories of peacebuilding in faraway places like Bosnia or Liberia they glamorize those situations and de-skill themselves by thinking that efforts for peace in civil wars are much more important than anything they do in their comparatively small lives. I ardently believe this is not true, for two reasons.

First, what happened in Bosnia or Kosovo is simply a more extreme version of what happens in our daily lives. As long as we maintain a separative, superior, or adversarial way of seeing the world and relating with others, we are engaged in our own civil wars. We may act more "civilly"—that is, we may not resort to bombs, bullets, and burning—

but we are, nonetheless, participating in and supporting systems and situations of conflict and suffering between parents and children, between ex-spouses, feuding friends, or factions at work. The work of mending the sacred hoop and remembering right relationship is the same, wherever we do it.

Second, in whatever setting we do our peacebuilding work, we are giving energy to the whole. Since we are one, each and every heart that opens, even a little bit, opens the one heart of us all. Since we are one, every strand of interconnectedness that is rewoven strengthens the fabric of all our lives. When even one of us experiences healing and forgiveness, the tide of love reaches to all of us on the shore.

The phenomenon of critical mass is not just a theory of physics for nuclear detonation. Critical mass operates on a social scale as well, through what has come to be known as the "Hundredth Monkey" phenomenon. Because we are connected in a single energy field, the learning that happens anywhere in the field is instantaneously translated throughout the entire field. So if I take the next step for me, in rebuilding trust with a loved one, or in creating a more positive environment in my work group, I am actually generating benefit for the entire universe; I am engaged in an act of generosity!

I am reminded of an advertising flyer I once received from a handyman. "No job too small!" it said, and that is my belief, too, when it comes to building peace.

The skill of risking the action is not as specific as the other skills we have discussed: centering home, meeting in the light, and letting go. Risking the action is unique to each person in each moment. The risk is different, the action is different, but the goal is the same: to grow peace in our lives and in the world.

There are several useful approaches to risking the action. The first is "bracketing the experience as an offering." From my Native American and Tibetan Buddhist teachers, I have learned the importance of dedicating my activities. If I begin an activity by offering it to the benefit of the whole circle of life, and if I do the same at the end of the day or at the end of the action, I am in effect releasing that action and whatever may unfold from it into a much larger realm, using the power of peace for a greater good than my own. I am amplifying whatever benefit may arise through my activities, and broadcasting that benefit throughout the web of life.

Another trick of the trade is, "When in doubt, move to a larger perspective." Because the part contains the whole, we have access to ever-greater levels of awareness from which to understand any situation. The first pictures of Earth from space made abundantly clear to all of us that, by drawing back to get a larger view, we change the whole framework of our understanding. In those pictures, there were no political boundaries apparent, no racial or religious differences. There was only one single fragile globe, sustaining one single fragile web of life.

We can do the same in all our activities. Often we get stuck because we are viewing things too narrowly. If we can step back and see a larger picture, or look from the next level of awareness, things are likely to seem different, and new possibilities will emerge. I have often sat in groups, for instance, where the verbal discussion was stuck, mired in minute details and differing opinions, so that a decision seemed impossible. When we stopped, took a deep breath and a moment of silent reflection to listen for the larger will of the group, inevitably new approaches became available, or the right next step became clear.

Unleashing the Power of Peace

Taking the larger view might mean asking ourselves what difference this will all make ten years from now. Or it might mean taking the time to reconnect with our purpose, so we can see if we're on the right track. If we are thinking about how some situation is affecting us, it may mean stepping back and asking how it might be affecting others as well. Or it may mean wondering what our mother, or our teacher, or some other person we respect would do in this situation.

Taking a larger view might also mean activating the third force— finding some element to bring into the situation that allows for the dynamics to shift from an adversarial to alliance mode. Or it may mean introducing some quality, like compassion or hope or inspiration, that actually raises the vibration of the encounter.

I once went walking by a remote stream in the mountains of Vermont. I came to a place of special beauty, with a serene pool surrounded by stately pines and ancient rocks. At the other side of the pool was a steep and surging waterfall. I desperately wanted to stand under it, and feel its power on my entire body. The only problem was, the water was bitterly cold, and I hate getting into cold water!

I dallied by the side of the pool for many minutes, thrusting a toe or two into the stream and drawing back quickly from the effect of the shocking cold on my thin blood. I wanted to go in, but I just couldn't bring myself to take that plunge. Then I had a strange thought. "What if," I mused, "Christ (or Buddha or God) were standing in that waterfall with arms wide open, saying, 'Come to me!' Would I hesitate?" Not for a second. I dove in, and swam to the waterfall, welcoming its majestic embrace.

A third approach to risking action involves making a safe space within which others can risk their action. The more we feel safe, the more we are willing to stretch beyond our comfort zone as a peace-builder. To know that we have permission to feel whatever we need to feel, and that we have the protection to do so as well, can allow us to take steps that would otherwise seem impossible. As a facilitator of numerous and various peacebuilding situations, I believe that the biggest contribution I can make is to provide safe space for the parties in conflict to do their work.

The safety I am referring to can be both physical and psychological. It radiates from inside me, and also results from the actions I take to insure that others can know they are in a setting where they will not be hurt or judged. Elizabeth Slade, a teacher from Ipswich, Massachusetts, tells a story about such a place.

There is an area in my classroom called the Peace Corner. It is sep-arated from the general flow of the room by a low bookshelf, and there is a glass door on one side for looking out at the world. In the Peace Corner there is a rug, a comfortable pillow, and a low table. On the table are things from nature, a Zen sand tray, and a few sim-ple items of beauty. Under the table is a class journal for writing or drawing. On the wall is a picture of the Earth, and quotations relat-ing to the subject of peace.

In our classroom community, anyone in the Peace Corner is left undisturbed. It is a place for solitude and personal reflection, where a student can go to have their feelings, to work, regroup, or mediate a difficult situation.

One day a student from another class was very angry. Jack was out in the hall, swinging his arms and shouting at everyone to leave him alone. His teacher was trying to get hold of him, which was intensifying Jack's reaction. I stepped out of my classroom into the hall, and my unexpected appearance changed the energy a little, while everyone took in my presence. Without allowing a moment to pass, I spoke directly to Jack. I told him that I had the perfect place for him to be left alone, and that he should follow me. I turned back to my classroom, letting him know I completely trusted that he would follow. He did.

Many people, when they hear about the Peace Corner, express doubt and fear that if there were such a place, the children would never want to leave it. My answer is twofold: first, if the classroom is as positive and nurturing a place as the Peace Corner, then there would be no reason for a child to make that choice. And second, if the students feel trusted to make that decision on their own, they will only be there for as long as they need to. Children inherently don't want to be cut off from others.

Within twenty minutes Jack emerged from the Peace Corner, his face tear-streaked, his energy subdued. I had my eye out for him, so I casually approached and asked if he wanted to hold one of our class pets. After he had a few minutes of cuddling with a furry friend, I sat with him. Then it was a good time to talk about what had been going on in the hall.

Jack visited my room several times that year. The next year our school integrated Peace Education into the curriculum. Now every class has a Peace Corner.

Over the last nine years I have watched many students find themselves and their equanimity as a direct result of having a place in the classroom that is delegated simply for that purpose. It is as though the very presence of this place within their environment validates and honors the work of becoming a centered person. I suppose it follows the idea of, "If you build it, they will come."

A fourth approach to risking action is to acknowledge successes of all sizes and appearances. The way we have defined peacebuilding here, it is actually a revolutionary or transformative process. That is, it seeks to change the very basis and norms of our societies, in which the "us" versus "them" mind of separation and dominance is deeply embedded in our institutions.

Our efforts to change this will prevail to the extent that a critical mass succeeds in growing a strong energy field of right relationship, an accomplishment that is supported by each and every act of peacebuilding. We need not be discouraged in this, thinking that our small step and tiny success is insignificant in the larger scale of the need. Every step counts. Every time any one of us lays down our sword or our shield, our inclination to attack or defend, and chooses instead to be present to the full power of the Spirit of Peace, the growing structure of a world in right relationship is strengthened.

Frank Blechman, a professor at the Institute for Conflict Analysis and Resolution at George Mason University, talks of working on large-scale public policy consensus-building, a process that may unfold over months or years. He sees that for every one or two steps forward there may be a step backward as well.

My students designed and facilitated a dialogue several years ago between Hispanic youth gang leaders and members of the county police anti-gang unit. By the seventh (of ten) sessions, the two groups were interacting well, having found many commonalties in their views about such things as the value of friends, the importance of being prepared, the need for discipline, and the virtue of uniforms.

The police were ecstatic. One reported before a dialogue session: "This weekend, I stopped a stolen car at 2 A.M. It was loaded with Hispanic youth. The driver immediately started screaming about how I was only stopping the car because the kids were brown. Seeing the other kids starting to pile out of the car, I feared trouble. Then, out of the back came one of the kids in the dialogue. He helped calm the others, telling them, 'Hey. Be cool. I know this guy.' We talked and the situation was handled without violence. It was great."

Frank goes on to note, however, that: "(1) Our hero is a gang kid, riding with six other gang members at 2 A.M Sunday morning in a stolen car; and (2) the policeman still had to arrest three of the kids for weapons and drugs, as well as for the car."

While the new trust in the relationship had averted violence, still the larger system in which this relationship was embedded hadn't changed that much. This may be true, but so is the fact that a melee between the gang members and the police was averted because of the fruits of a peacebuilding effort. The success of that deserves to be celebrated, and certainly would be by the families of those youth who didn't receive a phone call saying their child was in the hospital or the morgue. Of course it would be better if those youth also weren't in jail, but we can honor and acknowledge each small step.

I, for one, have faith that these small steps will eventually lead to a major transformation in how we live together, treat each other, and organize our societies. I have this faith because I know the Spirit of Peace is a vital presence in each of us, and I trust that when any one of us risks some action for peace, the Spirit of Peace becomes a bigger and stronger force in all our lives.

Unleashing the power of peace, then, means remembering that we are peacebuilders in every moment, through our thoughts, words, and deeds, and daring to step forward into actions, no matter how small they may seem, that will loose this power through our hearts and hands into the world around us.

When that action is grounded in a remembrance of our Oneness and a recognition that we belong to each other, and when it is directed toward opening the heart to mend what is broken, or to prevent further breaking of our precious circle of life, then truly we can say the Spirit of Peace is moving in our lives. Then truly we can say we are building a better world, through finding that better way. For the opportunity to participate as one small player in this glorious cosmic game, I am grateful.

Practice Risking the Action

Here are some ways to experience yourself as a peacebuilder in every moment, and practice the skills put forth in this chapter, skills of taking responsibility for doing what needs to be done for peace.

1. Meditative Practice for Risking the Action

Once again, align your body and breath with Source, centering home. Think about one incident, activity, or event recently in your life that you could describe as a successful step in peacebuilding, no matter how small or how large. Focus on one moment where your heart was opened in reconciliation, where an adversary became an ally, where you improved the quality of a relationship, where you found a creative or cooperative solution to a conflict, or any other such moment where the Spirit of Peace moved in you. Celebrate the success of that event! Feel the joy and satisfaction that comes with knowing you added your drop to the bucket. Breathe into it and magnify it, then send that joy out in a radiant stream of light, dedicating it to the service of others who are in need of peace in their lives. Make an offering of this success, sharing it with all your relations in the sacred circle of life, that they too might know the power of peace. What do you notice?

2. *Action Practice for Risking the Action*

Think of a conflict situation in your life in which you would like to practice being a peacebuilder. It can be something directly involving you, or something you witness between others. It can at the individual level or the international, or anything in between. Now write down at least seven possible actions you might take to make some contribution to peace in this situation. Pick one thing from your list, and do it, now. Risk the action.

Finding the Courage for Peace in the Twenty-First Century

THE MOMENT OF moving into a new millennium is an exciting one. Inevitably, we have the sense of stepping across an important threshold, into a space and time that stretches open before us for a hundred years and more, a period of great uncertainty and change. The past belongs to another era. How we will shape the twenty-first century and beyond depends on the seeds we plant now.

I recently attended religious services at a synagogue. I was struck by how much the liturgy spoke about peace in the abstract. During the service, I couldn't help but reflect on the distance between those noble-sounding ideals and the actual, relatively grim reality on the ground between Israelis and Palestinians.

Then, after the service, someone made an announcement about the Social Action Committee's program for racial justice, scheduled for that week. I felt heartened to see some effort to directly apply the spiritual teachings. Later I heard that at a study group meeting the next morning, a person of color in the congregation had shared his anger at hearing racist comments and jokes during the social gathering immediately after the services. This provided the group with the very concrete opportunity to work with the divisive prejudices existing in their own midst.

I enter the twenty-first century with great hope for peacebuilding because of this story—not, of course, because of this one incident alone, but because it typifies a growing phenomenon in our society. In our schools and neighborhoods; in our churches, mosques, temples, and synagogues; in our businesses and professions; even in the halls of government, media, and academia people are waking up to the need to find the Spirit of Peace.

I attribute this awakening to two related trends: a greater breakdown of worn-out systems and a greater awareness of our evolutionary potential. Writers, thinkers, activists, scientists, and political and religious figures have been pointing our attention for several years to the general unraveling of many of our systems. Though people name it differently, all are essentially naming a condition that I call "a loss of systemic integrity."

In the new diseases of our times, the cells cannot hold their integrity. Previously unknown viruses proliferate. Frogs and other species are appearing in bizarre mutated forms. The very atmosphere of the planet is shredding, with a growing hole in the ozone layer.

Meanwhile, our youth grow up confused and alienated, without heroes and, increasingly, without stable home lives. Failing to distinguish between the fantasy of video games and the reality of flesh and blood, they take guns to school and murder classmates and teachers. In the United States, the world's greatest democracy and strongest economy, millions of people have nowhere to live but the streets, teachers cannot pass basic competency exams, and schools fall apart while prison construction flourishes.

In the international scene, many states are failing, politically, economically, or both. Extremism is growing in all sectors and religions, with a greater willingness to use terrorist tactics and violence to destroy opponents. National borders and legal mechanisms are unable to stop the flow of dirty money, the sex trade, drugs, and weapons. The global economy and the global communications net are increasingly vulnerable to massive disruption and meltdown.

People argue that these and similar symptoms are nothing more than the normal trials and tribulations of human society. I think otherwise. I think they are indicative of a larger event in planetary evolution. I believe we have reached the end of a particular evolutionary period, and have entered another. That this happens to correspond to the beginning of a new millennium, and that it entails periods of upheaval and confusion, makes complete sense to me.

We have lived within an intellectual and systemic worldview of reductionism for many centuries. That worldview, which seeks to reduce the universe to its constituent parts and understand its workings mechanistically, naturally favors a linear, rational, problem-oriented mode of thinking and a compartmentalized, separative, and dominance approach in social relations.

Simply put, this worldview, and all the systems established to preserve and promote it, have come to the end of their cycle. Seeking to impose a way of life that is not in harmony with the nature of reality, or natural law, this worldview has always carried within it the seeds of its own demise, and those seeds have now ripened.

Meanwhile, a new cycle is beginning, one that stems from the recognition of the fact that we are one. Favoring a relational, intuitional, opportunity-oriented way of thinking and a community, interconnective, partnership approach to social relations, this new way of being is built on our emerging understanding of universal truths: We cannot reduce things to the smallest piece of matter; matter is energy with meaning and motion. Life is not static; it is flow. We are not broken; we are whole. If we oppress others, we oppress ourselves.

A massive shift in consciousness is occurring across the planet, as more and more people recognize the truly holistic nature of our world. Expressed in various ways—the civil rights movement, the women's movement, increased environmental awareness, growing interest in Eastern and indigenous philosophies, the mainstreaming of holistic health approaches, attention to participatory teamwork and the role of spirit in the workplace, the new physics—this transformation in consciousness is the new wave that will carry us into the twenty-first century and beyond.

Even as the old systems disintegrate and fade away, pioneers among us are creating new ways of living and working together that honor the truth of our oneness. I happen to believe that peacebuilding is at the forefront of this wave, and that its pioneers are and will be among the greatest champions of a new era.

This is true for two reasons. First, the old does not necessarily give way to the new gracefully. Old systems die hard, with much kicking and screaming, retrenching and resistance. This produces greater stress and strife. In this growing arena of conflict, peacebuilders are the ones who can be effective. They are needed; they have the skills and the knowledge to make a difference; they can build bridges across the deepening chasms in our societies, as some people cling tenaciously to what is familiar, others rush into the promise of the unknown, and most of us mill around somewhere in the middle, lost in the confusion and vulnerable to manipulation.

Second, peacebuilders carry the template of the new era. By the very nature of its work, and the assumptions on which its work is based, peacebuilding is an inclusive, holistic, partnership-oriented process. It is the thread and the needle with which the broken hoop is mended.

The four spiritual principles I've been describing—unity, interrelatedness, love, and co-creativity—taken together are the map for our individual and collective journey into the future. They show us how to align our thoughts and actions with what is, allowing us to move in harmony with the evolutionary flow of these times, both hastening and grounding the new cycle of human consciousness.

On a more practical level, the four principles and the peacebuilding concepts and practices that derive from them are our tools for shaping the structures, systems, and relationships of the next century. They give us concrete direction in a time of flux, tangible methods in a time of uncertainty. They give us specific, clear guidance on what to do and how to do it, as we seek to live our lives as dignified human beings, in right relationship with others, near and far, with whom we share life on this precious planet.

I have tried to bring both inspiration and pragmatism to these pages. The times call for us to integrate our hearts and our hands, spirit and action, as we seek to build peace in a broken world. I have attempted to show the Spirit of Peace as a living process, encoded in our hearts, embodied in our words, expressed through our thoughts, and empowered through our choices. I hope I have been successful, for I believe the Spirit of Peace, as it moves in our lives, is the guardian angel of humanity's future in this period of profound transformation.

I pray that all the sacred circle of life will be strengthened through these simple words on paper, and through whatever actions these words might encourage in those who read them. I pray that this book may be a seed of hope and compassion to all who suffer the anguish of war, violence, hatred, abuse, or oppression, and a source of inspiration for all who would step forward in these times to live with the courage for peace.

May the Spirit of Peace reach through these pages and bless us all.

Call to Action:
Peace Resource Guide

YOU CAN DISPLAY your own courage for peace by getting involved in activities that create greater harmony in your life and in the world. The organizations listed are good places to start, but are only a very small sample of the resources and avenues available. You may be aware of programs or projects in your own community where you can join with others in the critical work of building a world of peace and nonviolence for all our relations.

International Year for the Culture of Peace

Now is an especially good time to get involved in peacebuilding activities, as the year 2000 has been officially designated by the United Nations as the International Year for the Culture of Peace. This year in turn will lead into a UN Decade for a Culture of Peace and Nonviolence for the Children of the World (2001–2010). There will be many special activities all over the world during these times, involving private citizens, local organizations, and governments. Find out how you can participate!

UNESCO

Washington, D.C.; phone: 202-331-9118; fax: 202-331-9121; e-mail: unesco2@cais.com; Web site: **www.unesco.org**. United Nations Educational, Scientific, and Cultural Organization (UNESCO) is the coordinating agency of this UN program. The Culture of Peace refers to the values, attitudes, and behaviors that reflect respect for life, for the rights and dignity of all beings, for the rejection of violence in all its forms, and for commitment to the principles of freedom, justice, solidarity, tolerance, and understanding among peoples and between groups and individuals. If you would like more information on ways in which you personally, or the institution you represent, can participate actively in celebrating the International Year for the Culture of Peace, contact the UNESCO office in Washington, D.C.

International Peacebuilding Programs

There are a growing number of organizations working in places of ethnic and civil war around the world, empowering people from all walks of life to get involved in breaking the cycle of violence and promoting reconciliation. Many of these are membership organizations, where members can participate by taking part in a larger set of worthwhile activities; others provide different avenues for active participation.

The Institute for Multi-Track Diplomacy (IMTD)

Washington, D.C.; phone: 202-466-4605; fax:202-466-4607; e-mail: imtd@imtd.org; Web site: **http://www.imtd.org**. IMTD takes a transformative, systems approach to peacebuilding around the world, helping people from all sectors of society find ways to step forward as responsible peacebuilders in their communities. With projects in many of the major tension spots of the world (including the Middle East, Bosnia, Cyprus, East and West Africa, India and Pakistan), IMTD is helping build a human and institutional infrastructure that can address the root causes of deeply entrenched social conflicts and help heal the wounds of war. IMTD has members in thirty-five countries, dedicated to supporting peacebuilding from the bottom up as well as the top down. IMTD has an extensive Occasional Paper series and offers professional development training programs for peacebuilders in the United States and abroad. Louise Diamond, the author of this book, is the cofounder and president of IMTD.

National Peace Foundation (NPF)

Washington, D.C.; phone: 202-223-1770, 1-800-237-3223; fax: 202 223-1718; e-mail: ntlpeace.org; Web site: **www. nationalpeace.org**. The National Peace Foundation is a private, nonpartisan, nonprofit membership organization with approximately 10,000 members nationwide. The Foundation's overall mission is to promulgate peacebuilding and conflict resolution at every level, from the community, to the regional, to the national and international. NPF organizes and carries out dialogues, seminars, and conflict resolution training and mediation programs in the United States and abroad. NPF and IMTD have recently formed an exciting new program, the Peacebuilders Partnership, as an umbrella program to promote cooperation among diverse individuals and groups involved with peacebuilding activities. Contact the NPF office to find out about this, their Adopt-a-School program, or their overseas projects.

Moral Rearmament (MRA)

Washington, D.C.; phone: 202- 872-9077; fax: 202-872- 9137; e-mail: mrawash@aol.com; Web site: **http://www.mra.org.uk**. MRA is an international network of people who work toward far-reaching change, locally and globally, by starting with change in their own lives. Beginning with the moral and spiritual response each of us can make to the needs of our world, MRA draws together people who do not usually work in partnership—across social, economic, religious and ethnic divides. From their homes, as well as through conferences, seminars, training courses, or some action to address a need in their community or country, they work as agents of change. MRA is open to all: contact them for more information about upcoming events around the world.

Mediation

You can learn to be a mediator, or bring a mediator in to manage a dispute in which you are a party, or find out more about this process that allows people to work out their differences cooperatively, with the help of a neutral third party.

Society of Professionals in Dispute Resolution (SPIDR)

Washington, D.C.; phone: 202-667-9700; fax: 202-265-1968; e-mail: spidr@spidr.org; Web site: **www.spidr.org**. SPIDR is a professional association of conflict resolvers (mediators, arbitrators, and other dispute resolution professionals) working at the local, regional, national, and international levels, through conferences, training institutes, and chapters. The group is committed to advance the highest standards of practice and ethics for dispute resolvers, to promote the understanding and widespread use of dispute resolution, and to encourage the widest possible diversity and multicultural expression within this field. Contact one of the twenty-plus local chapters listed on the Web site to find out how you can become involved.

The National Association for Community Mediation (NAFCM)

Washington, D.C.; phone: 202-467-6226; fax: 202-466-4769; e-mail: nafcm@nafcm.org; Web site: **www.nafcm.org**. NAFCM is a membership organization comprised of community mediation centers, their staff, volunteer mediators, and other individuals and organizations interested in the community mediation movement. One of the purposes of this group is to support the maintenance and growth of community-based mediation programs. NAFCM has ten regional offices, which can be reached by logging on to their Web site.

Mediation Information and Resource Center (MIRC)

http://www.mediate.com. This Web site provides excellent and thorough information on all aspects of mediation and conflict resolution, including online discussion groups and forums, training and academic programs, a newsletter, plus useful information on finding a mediator near you. Log on to find out how you can benefit and participate.

Youth Programs

In many school districts, conflict resolution and peer mediation are being practiced by both teachers and students. There is data to suggest that this training reduces school violence and behavioral problems, and that the children often take their new skills home to help change family dynamics. Many communities also have special programs focusing on the needs of youth, helping them find nonviolent responses to the stresses of life.

The Conflict Resolution Education Network (CREnet)

Washington, D.C.; phone: 202-667-9700; fax: 202-667-8629; e-mail: nidr@nidr.org; Web site: http://www.crenet.org. CREnet is the primary national and international clearinghouse for information, resources, and technical assistance in the field of conflict resolution and education. A 1997 estimate indicates that there are more than 8,500 school-based conflict resolution programs in the United States, located in the nation's 86,000 public schools, teaching and modeling the skills of mediation, negotiation, and collaborative problem solving. Underlying all of these processes is the philosophy that problems can be resolved in ways that benefit everyone involved. The most common conflict resolution programs are peer mediation programs. You can contact CREnet to find out how you can get conflict resolution programs in your school.

Educators for Social Responsibility (ESR)

Cambridge, Mass.; phone: 617-492-1764; fax: 617-864-5164; Web site: **www.esrnational.org**. The primary mission of ESR is to make teaching social responsibility a core practice in education so that young people develop the convictions and skills needed to shape a safe, sustainable, democratic, and just world. ESR is a leading source of innovative curriculum materials and teacher training programs focusing on issues of peacemaking and conflict resolution. It offers workshops, materials, conferences, and onsite training, plus special projects in a variety of educational settings. ESR's largest initiative, the Resolving Conflict Creatively Program, is a comprehensive K-12 school-based program in conflict resolution and intergroup relations for preventing violence and creating caring learning communities. Contact ESR to discover how its expertise might benefit your school or community.

National Youth Advocate Program

Washington, D.C.; phone: 202-244-6410; fax: 202-244-6396; e-mail: nyap@msn.com. The purpose of this program is to help youth work toward a safer community by controlling anger at home and at school, and by using nonviolent methods of conflict resolution. It also includes work with the family as a major educational component for safer, non-violent, gun-free homes. Call to see how you can become a mentor or an advocate for youth or families in your area.

Racial Harmony and Diversity

In most American cities there are local programs promoting racial harmony and honoring the rich diversity of our population. Many of these are sponsored by religious organizations, some by the municipalities themselves or by local grassroots organizations.

Hope In the Cities (National Coalition)

Richmond, Va.; phone: 804-358-1764; fax: 804-358-1769; e-mail: hopecities@aol.com; Web site: **www.hopeinthecities.org**. "Hope in the Cities" (HIC), first launched in 1990, is a twelve-city network that offers experience, resources, and a process to encourage reconciliation and responsibility for positive change on race relations. Through their Call to Community, a program that provides a demonstration of respectful public dialogue on race, HIC invites people to have honest conversations on race; to show acceptance of responsibility; and to conduct acts of reconciliation. Contact HIC to see if there are already programs in your area, or to find out how you might start one.

Search for Common Ground on Race

Washington, D.C.; phone: 202-265-4300; fax: 202-232-6718; e-mail: awind@sfcg.org; Web site: **www.sfcg.org**. Search for Common Ground on Race was launched in 1998 as an attempt to affect national discussion on race by joining liberal and conservative organizations in concrete projects related to race and affirmative action. The point of the program is to build on commonalities, rather than trying to persuade opposing groups to abandon their positions and reach a compromise. The goal is tangible, action-oriented projects rather than dialogue. This project is an active participant in the President's Initiative on Race. To learn more, or to offer ideas on projects that liberals and conservatives might agree upon, contact the program directly.

Academic Programs in Peace and Conflict Studies

It is increasingly possible to take college courses or to get advanced degrees in the subject of peace and conflict studies. Many people with those degrees are building a new professional base for this emerging field.

Institute for Conflict Analysis and Resolution (ICAR)

George Mason University, Fairfax, Va.; phone: 703-993-1300; fax: 703-993-1302; e-mail: icarinfo@osf1.gmu.edu; Web site: **www.gmu.edu**. The Institute for Conflict Analysis and Resolution offers Ph.D. and M.S. degrees in Conflict Analysis and Resolution. Both degrees support the Institute's mission, which is to advance the understanding and resolution of significant and persistent human conflicts among individuals, small groups, communities, ethnic groups, and nations. Major research interests include the analysis of deep-rooted conflicts and their resolution; the exploration of conditions attracting parties to the negotiation table; the role of third parties in dispute resolution; and the testing of a variety of conflict intervention methods in community, national, and international settings. Community outreach is accomplished through the publication of books and articles, public lectures, conferences, seminars, and special briefings on the theory and practice of conflict resolution. ICAR collaborates on a range of projects with other academic programs and practice organizations. Visit the Web site for admission requirements.

International Peace and Conflict Resolution Program (IPCR)

American University, Washington, D.C.; phone: 202-885-1622; fax: 202-885-1661; e-mail: peace@american.edu; Web site: **www.american.edu**. The multidisciplinary IPCR, housed in the School of International Service, is designed for undergraduate and graduate students and faculty concerned with understanding the causes of war and organized violence and constructing conditions for peace. The program explores the following critical issues: the causes of war and organized violence at the intranational and international levels; alternative approaches to resolving and preventing conflict; approaches to peacemaking; the formation of cooperative global relationships; crosscultural negotiation; and individual and community transformation. IPCR offers master's and Ph.D. degrees, as well as an undergraduate concentration in the discipline, plus intensive three-day trainings in conflict resolution techniques for degree and nondegree students through the Conflict Resolution Skills Institutes. Application material can be downloaded from the Web site.

Conflict Transformation Program (CTP)

Eastern Mennonite University, Harrisonburg, VA; phone: 540-432-4490, 1-800-710-7871; fax: 540-432-4449 or 540-432-4444; e-mail: CTProgram@emu.edu; Web site: **www.emu.edu/ctp/ctp.htm**. The Conflict Transformation Program was founded to further the personal and professional development of individuals as peacebuilders and to strengthen the peacebuilding capacities of the institutions they serve. The program is committed to supporting conflict transformation and peacebuilding efforts at all levels of society in situations of complex, protracted, violent, or potentially violent social conflict in the United States and abroad. Open to people from all parts of the world and all religious traditions, CTP is an outgrowth of the centuries-old Mennonite peace tradition rooted in the values of nonviolence, social justice, public service, reconciliation, personal wholeness, and appreciation for diversity of all types. CTP offers a Master's degree program, an eighteen-credit Graduate Certificate in Conflict Transformation, the Institute for Peacebuilding (IFP), which involves applied practice and research, and a Summer Peacebuilding Institute with specialized workshops specifically tailored for practitioners working in situations of protracted conflict. For more information contact the program office.

Advocacy and Activism

Private citizens can actively support the cause closest to their heart—whether it be peace and justice, human rights, or a stronger United Nations—by getting involved in one of the myriad activist organizations.

United Nations Association (UNA-USA)

New York, N.Y.: phone: 212-907-1300; fax: 212-682-9185; e-mail: unahq@unausa.org; Web site: **http://www.unausa.org**. UNA-USA is a nonprofit, nonpartisan national organization dedicated to enhancing U.S. participation in the United Nations system and to strengthening that system as it seeks to define and carry out its mission. UNA-USA's action agenda uniquely combines education and public research, substantive policy analysis, and ongoing U.S.-U.N. dialogue. With 23,000 members nationwide, UNA combines broad grassroots outreach with high-level policy studies involving scholars and government officials from many parts of the world in order to identify fresh ideas and areas of potential cooperation. There are more than 175 chapters and divisions throughout the country conducting a wide variety of activities, often in close cooperation with city and state governments, the media, area schools, and other local organizations. Contact the UNA headquarters in New York to get in touch with your closest UNA chapter.

Women's International League for Peace and Freedom (WILPF)

Philadelphia, Pa.; phone: 215-563-7110; fax: 215-563-5527; e-mail: wilpf@wilpf.org; Web site: **www.wilpf.org**. WILPF is the oldest and largest women's peace organization in the world. It was founded in 1915 at The Hague in protest of the First World War. Its purpose is to address the root causes of war such as militarism, racism, discrimination, intervention, and disparity in wealth. WILPF has several programs focused on women's rights, peace education, and racial justice and is represented in forty-four countries as well as in 110 cities in the United States. This global network of grassroots activist members works to create peace and justice from the community level to the international level.

Peace Action

Washington, D.C.; phone: 202-862-9740: fax: 202-862-9762; e-mail: pamembers@igc.org; Web site: **www.peace-action.org**. Peace Action is the nation's largest grassroots peace and justice organization, with affiliates in twenty-seven states and 100 local chapters across the United States. People from all walks of life, diverse racial and ethnic backgrounds, and many faiths share a commitment to a more peaceful and just world. Peace Action helps focus citizen activism on elected officials regarding such issues as abolishing nuclear weapons; eliminating Pentagon waste, fraud, and abuse to fund community needs; and ending U.S. weapon sales to human rights abusers. Its members organize, educate, and take part in nonviolent action to achieve its goals. Check with the office for the affiliate closest to you, or to participate in their national campaigns and programs.

Amnesty International

New York, NY; phone: 212-807-8400; e-mail: amnesty@igc. org; Web site: **www.amnesty.org**. Amnesty International (AI) is a worldwide campaigning movement to promote human rights. It particularly addresses such issues as freeing prisoners of conscience; ensuring fair and prompt trials for political prisoners; abolishing the death penalty, torture, and other cruel treatment of prisoners; and ending political killings and "disappearances." AI has a million members and supporters in 162 countries and territories. Activities range from public demonstrations to letter writing, from human rights education to fund-raising concerts, from individual appeals on a particular case to global campaigns on a particular issue. Contact the office to find out how you can join in the work of supporting human rights around the world.

Nonviolence

Most of us can agree that violence is not the way to solve our problems. But how to actively practice nonviolence is a question we need to approach pragmatically. Many organizations offer programs where we can learn and act in consciously nonviolent yet effective ways to reduce tension and witness for peace.

Alternatives to Violence Project (AVP)

Phone: 318-797-1412; e-mail: avp@avpusa.org; Web site: **www.avpusa.org**. Alternatives to Violence is a nationwide and worldwide association of volunteer groups offering experiential workshops in conflict resolution, responses to violence, and personal growth. Dedicated to reducing the level of violence in our society, AVP offers training especially in those places where violence is often found, most especially prisons, schools, and communities. AVP seeks to encourage people to lead nonviolent lives and to realize their innate power to positively transform themselves and the world. Contact their office to find AVP programs near you.

Fellowship of Reconciliation (FOR)

Nyack, N.Y.; phone: 914-358-4601; fax: 914-358-4924; e-mail: for-natl@igc.org; Web site: **non-violence.org/nvweb/for**. Fellowship of Reconciliation is part of an international association of people of all faiths united in a vision of justice and reconciliation, and a search for concrete alternatives to violence. The U.S. branch has seventy local groups working to replace violence, war, racism, and economic injustice with nonviolence, peace, and justice. An interfaith group, the organization also facilitates the work of fifteen faith-based groups, such as the Jewish Peace Fellowship, the Buddhist Peace Fellowship, and the Muslim Peace Fellowship. FOR engages in education, training, building coalitions, and nonviolent and compassionate actions locally, nationally, and globally. It also offers a Peacemaker Training Institute to help young people become more effective peace and justice activists. Find out how you can be part of this exciting network that thinks globally and acts locally.

The Non-violence Web

Web site: **www.non-violence.org**. This unique Web site is the Internet home for many of the U.S.'s most dynamic peace groups. Here you can read issue pages discussing current events or critical issues facing the world community, or join an online discussion group on topics of particular interest. Or you can browse through the listings of peace and nonviolence organizations and programs to find the one that calls you to action.

Acknowledgments

THE SPIRIT OF PEACE has inspired, guided, and supported me in the writing of this book through many dear friends and helpers. In particular, I would like to acknowledge and shower with appreciation:

John McDonald, my partner and colleague at the Institute for Multi-Track Diplomacy, whose profound wisdom has grounded me deeply in the art and skill of peacebuilding, and whose encouragement and support over the years has made it possible for me to do this work; all the staff and interns at the Institute who kept things going so I could finish this book; and all my peacebuilding partners and friends around the world who, by inviting me into their homes and hearts, have blessed me with some small insight into what it really means to stand for peace in a place of war.

Also, Tiny Hoffman, who graciously shared her heart and home so that I might have an exquisite writing retreat on the Maine coast; Wendy Walsh and Jerielle Young, who feasted me shamelessly with their rare and unconditional love in countless forms; Marji Greenhut, my beach buddy, who kept me joyously in-sane; Jonathan Reitman, who graciously opened the door of invitation to bring me home to Maine; Kathleen Norris and others who lovingly cared for my precious physical and spiritual well-being while I was writing; my dearest friends Nina and Richard, cherished traveling companions of my soul; and the many other friends and spiritual family who daily held me in their prayers.

Also, Dawna Markova, who so generously brought me to Conari Press; Mary Jane Ryan, publisher and editor *par excellence;* and everyone at Conari who saw the potential of this book and went all out for it.

Finally, and especially, my beloved daughter Molly, who is, simply, the light of my life and one incredible woman!

About the Author

Louise Diamond is a writer, consultant, and educator whose passion is peace. She works as a professional peacebuilder in places of ethnic conflict around the world, and leads social change projects that promote peace-full societies.

Louise is the founder and CEO of The Peace Company, dedicated to making peace the way we live. The Peace Company (www.thepeace company.com) works for a culture of peace by offering products and services to inspire, inform, and engage people in creating peace in their own lives and in the world around them. It also seeks to lay the groundwork for a peace economy by demonstrating that peace is good business.

She is the author of several books on peace, including *The Peace Book: 108 Simple Ways to Make a More Peaceful World*. This book has sold over 65,000 copies through a unique initiative called **The Great Peace Give-Away**, where people buy multiple copies of the book from The Peace Company and give them away as gifts of peace to friends, colleagues, family, schools, etc. Other recent initiatives include a workbook on *How to Raise a Peaceful Child in a Violent World* (with co-author Elizabeth Slade), and **Zones of Peace**—a call for people from all walks of life to make peace a living presence in their own home, workplace, school, faith congregation, or other settings.

Louise is an internationally known trainer, public speaker, conference presenter, and peace champion who finds her own inner peace at home in the Green Mountains of Vermont. She can be reached at diamond@ thepeacecompany.com, and welcomes your comments on this book.